Making More Money

OTHER CAREER BOOKS
by Joyce Slayton Mitchell

I Can Be Anything: Careers for Young Women
The Men's Career Book: Work and Life Planning for a New Age
The Work Book: A Guide to Skilled Jobs
Free to Choose: Decision Making for Young Men
Stopout! Working Ways to Learn
The Classroom Teacher's Workbook for Career Education
See Me More Clearly: Career and Life Planning for Teens with Physical Disabilities
Taking on the World: Empowering Strategies for Parents of Children with Disabilities
Be a Mother and More: Career and Life Planning
Choices and Changes: A Career Book for Men
Computer-age Jobs: The Computer Skills You Will Need to Get the Job You Want
My Mommy Makes Money
From College to Career

Making More Money

55 SPECIAL JOB-HUNTING STRATEGIES FOR RETIREES

Joyce Slayton Mitchell

PRENTICE HALL PRESS • NEW YORK

Copyright © 1986 by Joyce Slayton Mitchell
All rights reserved, including the right of reproduction
in whole or in part in any form.

Published by Prentice Hall Press
A Division of Simon & Schuster, Inc.
Gulf+Western Building
One Gulf+Western Plaza
New York, NY 10023

PRENTICE HALL PRESS is a trademark of Simon & Schuster, Inc.

Library of Congress Cataloging-in-Publication Data

Mitchell, Joyce Slayton.
  Making More Money

    1. Job hunting—United States. 2. Aged—
Employment—United States. I. Title.
HF5382.75.U6M58   1987   650.1′4′0240564   86-12268
ISBN 0-13-417908-0

Manufactured in the United States of America

10 9 8 7 6 5 4 3 2 1

First Edition

To Sarah Arkin Slayton,
my courageous mother, who at 80 continues to teach me
most about the joy of living

Acknowledgments: Thanks Be to Others

I've never met so many people who wanted to help with a book. Going to Washington to collect the facts about older workers, to collect information about the needs of retirees from their associations and agencies and talking to the people throughout the country who have been teaching special job-hunting strategies for years turned out to be a cooperative effort which calls for my heartiest thanks.

I begin my thanks to others with my colleague and Vermont's renown advocate of older folks, Faire Edwards, who advised me not to make a move until I had met Dr. Robert N. Butler, the former director of the National Institute on Aging (1982), and had read his book, *Why Survive?*

Thanks be to Pearl Somaini-Dayer, the Washington-Vermonter who was the executive director of the Urban Elderly League, and introduced me to Arthur Fleming, considered the grandfather of the Commission on Aging.

8 • ACKNOWLEDGMENTS

On to the famous American Association of Retired Persons (AARP), where librarian Jo-Ellen Vernali-Knoerl works in the best library in town. She always found the next publication or special person I should see at the AARP. Dr. Paul Kershner, former associate director of the AARP, now head of the National Foundation for Long Term Health Care, always had time for *Making More Money*. Most recently, many thanks to the Work Force Education staff, who provided me with story-swapping from senior employment agencies and workshops for older workers.

At the National Council on the Aging, it's Lorretta Aiken, administrative assistant, whom I want to thank. She never tires of my questions, sending me the latest programs for employment. She first introduced me to Dorothy C. Bauer, and then to Don Davis, associate director of the council. Dorothy C. Bauer is now the president of the National Association of Mature People, but at the NCOA, she has done the most work in the nation on training workshops for older workers' employment.

The famous and oldest Senior Personnel Employment Council in America is in White Plains, New York. There, John J. Blanchfield was a major contributor through his sharing of the council's job files, the special communication tips he has learned from experience, and his advice to get on with *Making More Money* as fast as I could.

ACKNOWLEDGMENTS • 9

Thanks also to Merrell M. Clark, president of Elderworks of New York City; Dr. Malcolm H. Morrison, chief, research support staff for the United States Department of Labor; Anne Kohl, Bureau of Labor Statistics and specialist in employment for the older worker; and PJ Haduch, my encouraging editor at Prentice Hall Press.

My thanks, too, goes to workshop participants across the country who experienced the development of these 55 special job-hunting strategies and taught me best what goes into getting a job—at any age.

Thanks, with love, to my retired friends who continually teach me about life-long learning, Marge Behrens, Catherine East, Natalie Shepard, and my just-retired aunt, Eunice Marshall.

Finally, thanks be to my parents who taught me the New England work ethic and the joy of living that makes it worthwhile. My father was a wonderful example of figuring out how best to live, and working just enough to pay for it. *Making More Money* is dedicated to my mother who taught her three children how much food adds to a family and to life—especially in season—and how much better it tastes in a beautiful home. Her children are proud of her as she continues her independent quest: all on her Social Security check, a little job here and there during her 70s, and in her original Vermont home, that she decided not to sell after all.

Contents

Basic Beliefs	17
It's the Law: Social Security	19
Count Your Blessings	21
Blessed Assurance	37

PART I

WHAT CAN YOU DO?

18 Special Self-assessment Strategies for Retirees

STRATEGY 1	A Transferable Skills List	41
2	Identifying Transferable Skills	47
3	Identifying Your Strongest Transferable Skills	49

STRATEGY 4 Documenting Your Transferable Skills — 51

5 A Job Skills List — 53

6 Identifying Your Job Skills — 56

7 Identifying More Job Skills — 58

8 Documenting Job Skills — 60

9 Identifying Your Interests — 62

10 What Activities Do You Enjoy? — 65

11 Changing Interests — 67

12 Clarifying Values — 69

13 Job Values List — 72

14 Job Values Exercise — 74

15 Ideal Job — 78

16 Long-range Goal Setting — 80

17 Plan of Action — 81

18 Timetable — 83

PART II

WHERE ARE THE JOBS?
26 Special Job-researching Strategies for Retirees

STRATEGY
- **19** Create a Job Possibilities List — *87*
- **20** Senior Employment Agency Jobs — *89*
- **21** Senior Agency's Easiest Jobs to Fill — *94*
- **22** Senior Agency's Hardest Jobs to Fill — *96*
- **23** Largest Number of New Jobs — *98*
- **24** Where Are the Jobs? — *100*
- **25** Companies with Special Programs for Older Workers — *102*
- **26** State Office on the Aging — *109*
- **27** State Job Service — *121*

14 • CONTENTS

STRATEGY

28	Private Employment Agencies	123
29	Private Employment Service for Older Workers	124
30	Operation ABLE	132
31	Urban League	134
32	Nonprofit Employment Agencies for Older Workers	136
33	Yellow Pages	148
34	Newspaper Want Ads	149
35	Trade and Professional Journal Want Ads	150
36	No Agency/No Help Strategy	151
37	Civic and Government Business Organizations	153
38	Start Your Own Business	154
39	Research Your Job Possibilities List	159
40	Business Research	161

CONTENTS • 15

STRATEGY *41* Trade Journals *162*

42 Professional Associations *163*

43 People Research *164*

44 Work Experience *167*

PART III
HOW DO I GET WHAT I WANT?
11 Special Communication Skills for Retirees

STRATEGY *45* TempsAmerica's Communication Tips *173*

46 New York State Employment Service: Tips for Older Workers *175*

47 More Communication Tips *179*

48 Telephone Calls *182*

49 Filling Out the Job Application Form *184*

STRATEGY **50** Writing the Résumé: Selling You! *187*

51 Résumé Cover Letter *191*

52 Watch Your Body Language! *193*

53 Typical Interview Questions *194*

54 Managing the Interview *196*

55 You've Got It All Together! *204*

Basic Beliefs

- You are your own best resource

- Ability is ageless

- Making money feels good

- Experience is a valuable asset

- There is a job for you

- Flexibility is crucial for success

- Think and talk about experience, not age

It's the Law: Social Security

1. Under the new law, effective January 1985, Social Security beneficiaries who are 70 years old or older can get full Social Security benefits regardless of how much they earn in a year. In other words, if you are 70 years old or older, the sky's the limit on your earnings!

2. Under the new law, you can receive all benefits due you for the year if your earnings do not exceed the annual exempt amount. This amount was $7,320 for people who were between 65 and 70 years of age, and this will be increased each year as wage levels rise. That means if you are 65 years old, but not yet 70, you will be able to earn as much as $7,320 without losing any of your present Social Security benefits.

3. If you earn more than $7,320 and are 65 to 70 years old, only half of the amount over

$7,320 will be charged against your Social Security benefits. In other words, if you earn $10,000, only $1,340 will be held from your benefits, half of the difference between $7,320 and $10,000.

Count Your Blessings

WHAT ARE YOU WORTH?

Before you know how much money you need to earn to make ends meet, you will need to know how much money you've got and how much money you spend. What are your assets; what are you worth? What will it take for you to thrive? What will it take to make more money for a *quality* life?

COUNT YOUR BLESSINGS IN FOUR EASY STEPS

Insurance companies, stockbrokers, the American Association of Retired Persons (AARP), banks, and books are full of good suggestions and charts to help you figure out what you are worth. If you don't have a good idea of how much money you need to earn to make ends meet, here is a simple plan to get started. Count your blessings in four easy steps:

1. Add up your total income.
2. Figure out your total fixed expenses.
3. Estimate how much you need for daily expenses.
4. Balance your first three steps; that is, subtract total expenses from total income.

Step 1: Add Up Your Total Income

To start, don't get anxious because we're talking about money and numbers. Your answer doesn't have to be "perfect" or "right." This exercise is just for you. All you need is a ballpark figure from which to plan your future. Write down all the cash you expect to receive in the next 12 months. If your income is from wages or salary, include only take-home pay. If it is from your own business, farm, or free-lance work, make the best possible guess.

Add other cash income you expect to receive, such as interest or dividends from bonds and other investments, veteran's benefits, proceeds from life insurance or Social Security, rents, and money contributed by other family members. Add up and divide by 12, and you will see what your average money income will be for the next year. This is the money that you will have to save and spend.

Step 1 looks like this: On a separate sheet of paper, make monthly columns across the top, and down the side enter the categories in the following list (use the sample table on page 32).

A. Wages
   1. Net take-home pay on a monthly basis
   2. Continuation salary, fees, deferred income from own business
   3. Other business income

B. Pension Plans
   1. Social Security
   2. Company pension plans
   3. Keogh Plan or IRA
   4. Veteran's Administration benefits

C. Interest
   1. Annuities
   2. Savings
   3. United States, corporate, and other bond interests
   4. Interest from mortgages
   5. Interest from loans held

D. Profits
   1. Profits from sale of real estate, stocks, bonds, other investments
   2. Rents and royalties
   3. Expected new income

Step 2: Figure Out Your Total Fixed Expenses

Write down all of your fixed expenses: rent or mortgage payments, life insurance premiums (if you are still paying them—you shouldn't be if you are retired!), taxes other than those taken out of your pay, contributions, and installment payments. Again, take a separate sheet of paper, write the months across the top, and enter the following categories along the side (use the sample table on page 33).

   A. Fixed expenses
      1. Rent or mortgage including monthly pro-rate of property tax and insurance
      2. Utilities (water, electricity, gas, telephone)
      3. Car operation, maintenance, repair, insurance
      4. Insurance, other than car
         a. health
         b. life
      5. Installment contracts and required monthly payments
         a. automobile
         b. household items
         c. personal loans
      6. Support obligations under court order

Step 3: Estimate Your Daily Living Expenses

Most people don't know exactly how much it costs them to live on a daily or monthly basis. But with some thought, you can probably make some good guesses. Take a separate sheet of paper; if it's easier to figure your daily expenses by the week you can do it that way and multiply by four, or go ahead and make your monthly columns and enter your good guess for daily expenses by the month. Here are the categories to write on the side of the paper (use the sample table on page 34).

A. Daily living expenses
   1. Food
      a. at home
      b. eating out
   2. Clothing
   3. Transportation
      a. gas and oil
      b. bus or train
   4. Routine medical and dental
   5. Laundry and dry cleaning
   6. Recreation
   7. Entertainment
   8. Personal allowances (magazines, books, records, gifts, incidentals)

9. Other daily or weekly expenses—itemize
   a. _____
   b. _____
   c. _____

Step 4: Your Balance Sheet

Total Step 1: Fixed income
Total Step 2: Fixed expenses
Total Step 3: Daily expenses

Use a separate sheet of paper for your balance sheet (use the example on page 35). Subtract your total expenses from your income. Now you have a working idea of your blessings—what you are worth. Adding income and subtracting expenses on your balance sheet will be the basis for figuring next year's financial needs and what your income goal will have to be to make ends meet.

Your balance sheet tells you the difference between your income and your expenses. Besides that, most retirees have assets, such as their home, car, art work, jewelry, and furnishings. When they total their assets, many people find they are worth more than they thought they were—not that you would sell any of your assets, but then again, you might. But when you count your blessings you want as complete a picture as you can get. You need to be able to plan what assets you can cash in if you decide you need the money more than the asset. You may decide you need a smaller house or an apartment, and knowing how much you could get for your present house or apartment is a first step in making any changes. If you don't know the current market value of your home or car, call a local real estate agent or car dealer to get a clear estimate. It doesn't have to be exact; you only need a rough idea of your worth. Take another sheet of paper now and write down the following property assets, using the format below.

A. Deposit amounts
   1. Checking account $_____
   2. Savings and loan $_____
   3. Credit union $_____

B. Automobiles
   1. Year, make, and model $_____
   2. Year, make, and model $_____

C. Real estate
   1. Address and description $_____
   2. Address and description $_____

D. Household
   1. Furniture $_____
   2. Furnishings $_____

    3. Art $_____
    4. Equipment $_____

E. Securities
    1. Stocks—itemize $_____
    2. Bonds—itemize $_____

F. Life insurance
    1. Cash value $_____
    2. Cash value $_____

G. Other major assets
    1. _____ $_____
    2. _____ $_____
    3. _____ $_____

Now you have it. You have an estimate of your income, your expenses, and your assets. From this information you can get credit, you can feel secure, and you can change the information as you change your living situations. Many people like to figure their assets and just let them sit there, spending only the interest earned on their assets. Other retirees decide to spend some of their assets: cashing stocks and/or insurance policies and using a percentage of their assets for daily living expenses. Still others want to earn new money for their daily expenses, rather than spend any of their assets. Whichever way you decide to handle your finances, it's good to know how much you have in assets whether you use any of them for daily expenses or not.

Now that you have worked on the dollars and cents of your worth, keep in mind that earning money is not the only way to make ends meet. Not spending what you already have is usually easier than finding new money. It may help you to know that everybody feels—no matter what their income and assets—that they need more money to manage well. But money is not always the answer to security. What is often just as important is how you plan your budget and how you spend your money; how you look at and use your resources; how you make your assets work for you; and how you value your greatest asset—your ability to make money.

There are all kinds of ways to cut expenses to make ends meet. No one can tell you what your lifestyle ought to be and what choices you ought to make. Only you can decide how your income and assets are spent, how your resources are used. Do you spend on traveling? On giving to your children, to your grandchildren? On clothes? On eating out? How you make ends meet will depend on the way you choose to live and the goals you plan to achieve. Whatever brings greatest pleasure to you is where your priorities lie. Spend your money for what makes *you* feel good! Think about where you are now and where you will want to be three years and five years from now. Age is not a factor in planning ahead. Budgets and investments don't work on a day-at-a-time philosophy. Your money plan will change as your life situation changes. You are paying attention to making more money in order to have the money to spend as you want it—not to let money slip away, spending on things that you really aren't that crazy about.

Are you all set? Do you have an estimate of what you are worth? Do you have an idea of your monthly and yearly expenses? Can you see that a job bringing in $4,000 or $5,000 or $7,000 a year would be just the thing to make ends meet for you? Can you reach your income goal by working part time? By sharing a job? Or on a seasonal job, temporary job, just weekends, or by working at home?

Start now with Special Job-Hunting Strategy 1 to find the job that is going to provide you with your own independent way to make more money. The jobs are there. Your experience is an asset. Your ability to work is the best resource you have, regardless of your age.

Look now for a job that will provide you with just the right amount of money you need and just the right amount of working time you need to add interest and companionship to your life. These are *your* retirement years, and they are worth planning so you can get what you want.

WHAT ARE YOU WORTH?

STEP 1
TOTAL INCOME 198_

	Jan.	Feb.	Mar.	Apr.	May	June	July	Aug.	Sept.	Oct.	Nov.	Dec.
A. Wages												
B. Pension												
C. Interest												
D. Profits												

WHAT ARE YOU WORTH?

STEP 2:
TOTAL FIXED EXPENSES 198__

	Jan.	Feb.	Mar.	Apr.	May	June	July	Aug.	Sept.	Oct.	Nov.	Dec.
A. Fixed Expenses												
1. Rent												
2. Utilities												
3. Car												
4. Insurance												
a) health												
b) life												
5. Installments												
a) auto												
b) household												
c) loans												
6. Support												

WHAT ARE YOU WORTH?
STEP 3
DAILY LIVING EXPENSES (A GOOD GUESS) 198_

	Jan.	Feb.	Mar.	Apr.	May	June	July	Aug.	Sept.	Oct.	Nov.	Dec.
A. Daily Living												
1. Food												
a) at home												
b) eating out												
2. Clothing												
3. Transportation												
4. Laundry												
5. Recreation												
6. Entertainment												
7. Personals												
a)												
b)												
c)												
8. Other												
a)												
b)												
c)												

WHAT ARE YOU WORTH?

STEP 4
BALANCE SHEET

Total from Step 2: Fixed expenses $ _____
Total from Step 3: Daily expenses $ _____

                Add total expenses $ _____

Total from Step 1: Fixed income $ _____
Total expenses minus above $ _____

                Your net worth $ _____

Blessed Assurance

Use your best resource—your ability to work—to be assured that you can make more money. Follow the 55 Special Job-hunting Strategies for Retirees in order to find out

1. What you can do
2. Where the jobs are
3. How to get the job you want

PART I

WHAT CAN YOU DO?

18 Special Self-assessment Strategies for Retirees

STRATEGY 1

A Transferable Skills List

Ask yourself these questions: What can I do? What do I like to do? What do I know how to do? What are my abilities? Then, think about your achievements and your work experience in your home or work place and in your community. Learning to identify your skills is a crucial first step in finding your best job possibilities. What you can do and how well you enjoy the activity is an important part of getting a job.

   Transferable skills are the basic skills that everybody has—skills that people use over and over again in a great variety of activities and places. Speaking, writing, decision making, for example, are transferable skills. Transferable skills are learned everywhere. Persuasiveness, for instance, can be learned when you sell shoes, when you sell an idea for raising money, or when you try to sell your three-year-old grandchild a nap.

As you read the following list you will be able to identify your own transferable skills. Keep in mind as you read through the list that it doesn't matter where you learned the skill. It *does* matter that you have had experience with the particular skill. The skill must be something you can say you have experienced rather than something you think about or just fantasize about liking to do. Reading through the list will give you an idea of the great range of skills that it is possible to have. Each combination of skills that you have is what makes you unique. The way you put your transferable skills together is the way you will appear to the person you hope will hire you for the job.

TRANSFERABLE SKILLS

Administer programs
Advise people
Analyze data
Appraise services
Arrange social functions
Assemble apparatus
Audit financial records
Budget expenses

WHAT CAN YOU DO? • 43

Calculate numerical data
Check for accuracy
Classify records
Collect money
Compete with others
Compile statistics
Compose a letter
Compose a song
Confront other people
Cooperate with others
Coordinate events
Cope with complex programs
Cope with difficult people
Correspond with others
Counsel others
Create new ideas
Decide uses of money
Delegate responsibility
Design a plan or project
Display artistic ideas
Distribute products
Dramatize ideas
Drive cars and vans
Edit publications
Endure long hours
Endure slow work
Entertain people
Evaluate programs
Exhibit plans

Express feelings
Find information
Follow through on ideas
Handle complaints
Handle detailed work
Influence others
Initiate new solutions
Inspect physical objects
Instruct others, instruct self
Interpret languages
Interview people
Invent ideas
Investigate problems
Listen to others
Locate information
Manage an organization
Manage time
Mediate between people
Meet the public
Motivate others
Negotiate
Organize people and jobs
Persistence
Persuade others
Plan agendas
Plan organizational needs
Prepare materials
Print
Promote change

Promote events
Protect property
Question others
Raise funds
Read material
Record scientific data
Recruit people
Remember facts
Repeat facts and information
Research in library
Research in newspapers
Review programs
Run a meeting
Sell ideas
Sell products
Serve others
Set goals
Set up demonstrations
Share work and credit
Sketch charts and diagrams
Solve problems
Speak in public
Supervise others
Take risks
Teach people
Tolerate commotion
Tolerate interruptions
Tolerate noise
Train animals

46 • MAKING MORE MONEY

Update files
Visualize new ideas and procedures
Work with precision
Write clear reports
Write for publication

Can you add others to this list?

_____
_____
_____
_____

STRATEGY 2

Identifying Transferable Skills

You've read the list of transferable skills. As you read through the list you must have noticed that some seemed to apply to you, and others just didn't ring a bell. You are going to read through the transferable skills list (Strategy 1) again, and this time you are going to write down each of your skills. Now is a good time to start a job-hunting notebook. You can flip the pages of such a notebook back and forth, using all of your strategies as you go along, and you will always know where to find your special strategies. There they'll be, all together, in one place in your job-hunting notebook.

Starting with Strategy 2 in your job-hunting notebook, identify each of the skills that you possess. Be sure to add any other transferable skills you have that are not on the list. Don't be modest—this is the time to write down as many skills as you can. If in doubt, write it down; you can think more about it later. At this point make up the longest list of transferable skills that you can think of.

STRATEGY 3

Identifying Your Strongest Transferable Skills

Look at your long list of transferable skills. Now you are going to identify which are your strongest skills; which ones you do best. One way to figure out your strongest skills is to think of some activity that has made you proud, made you happy, made you excited. Think about the activities that give you energy. Identify the skills you use to make this happen, the abilities you have and use for this joyful activity. For example, if you were very proud of winning a sales contest, you could identify your transferable skills as follows: competing with others, analyzing, following through with ideas, handling details, influencing others, interviewing people, listening to others, negotiating, and persuading others by your sales ability. If you felt good about your record of walking two miles a day for two weeks, you could write persistence, self-discipline, and goal setting for your transferable skills. If you were very proud of your hospital volunteer work, your skills might include cooperating with others, coping with difficult people, expressing feelings, meeting the public, and being a good listener.

The identification of your strongest transferable skills is what you will use in determining what job you want, for writing your résumé, and for your interview. Even as you identify your strongest transferable skills, keep in mind that you will be constantly learning new skills as you gain new experiences. There is no age limit for learning new skills. Skills are ever changing. If you can't get started on identifying your transferable skills, ask your family and friends to help you. The more you know about your skills, the more easily you can decide what it is you want to do.

STRATEGY 4

Documenting Your Transferable Skills

It was easy to write the list, right? Now comes the hard part. You are going to prove or document that those strongest transferable skills you identified in Strategy 3 are really yours.

Using your strongest transferable skills list, write a note or phrase beside each skill in your job-hunting notebook to show how you used the skill or where you learned it. In other words, note how you can demonstrate that you have that particular ability and skill.

This is the time to come up with the evidence. This is the chance to prove your skills by documenting each one with some activity you have experienced. For example, writing is a transferable skill that may be on your list. What activities can you name that illustrate that you have this skill? Maybe you contributed to a newsletter? Or maybe you applied for a grant? Or maybe you can show your skill at writing brochures for a group you belong to? Let's take another one—cooperating with others. Again, find a life experience that proves your skill, for example, playing cards in a bridge club, working on a department project, or contributing to a book-reading club.

Go through your strongest transferable skills list (Strategy 3), noting one or two or three actions beside each skill that illustrate that skill. Remember, the activity can be one that you did at home, at school, as paid work, in the military, the nursery, or the community. Every place counts for learning transferable career skills.

STRATEGY 5

A Job Skills List

Now that you have identified and documented your transferable skills, the next step is to consider your job skills.

Job skills are specific skills used in particular places. Think of them as technical or specialized skills. Driving a car, for example, or typing, filling teeth, word processing, cooking, playing a clarinet, speaking French, or repairing a refrigerator are all job skills. Usually these skills are learned through a formal program at school; in an apprenticeship program; in a course, seminar, or workshop; on the job; or self-taught through a correspondence course or a reading program. Some examples follow.

JOB SKILLS

Accounting
Acting
Baking
Bookkeeping
Broadcasting
Casting Tool-and-Die molds
Cooking
Counseling
Cutting hair
Dancing
Data processing
Designing
Designing financial plans
Dressmaking
Driving a car
Driving a tractor or trailer
Dry cleaning
Editing
Filing
Firefighting
Fitting glasses
Key making
Landscaping
Marketing a product or concept
Navigating
Photography
Piano tuning

Playing a musical instrument
Playing a sport
Plumbing
Preparing a legal action
Printing
Selling a specific product or concept
Sign lettering
Speaking a foreign language
Teaching a particular subject
Technical writing
Telephone Operator
Treating sick animals
Treating sick people
Typing
Welding
Word processing
X-raying

Can you add others to this list?

_____
_____
_____
_____

STRATEGY 6

Identifying Your Job Skills

Make a list of your job skills. Think about skills you have learned at school. Did you learn how to repair a car? How to type, build a room, weld, manage money, cook, speak a foreign language, operate a saw, sew, install an electrical system, develop photographs?

If you were a college student, did you learn job skills in business, music, engineering, medicine, law, or agriculture? Liberal arts students probably developed transferable skills and then went on to specialize in job skills at graduate school, in a training program, or on the job. Did you get any job skills in the military? When you were at home with your children, did you read about child rearing and discuss it with other parents and child-care workers besides observing your own children? Did you learn daily-living job skills at home? How to cook, market, plan a budget? Be sure to include apprenticeship skills and any seminar, workshop, or on-the-job training programs you have been in.

STRATEGY 7

Identifying More Job Skills

Besides thinking about programs, you may be able to get some more clues about your job skills by looking at your list of strongest transferable skills (Strategy 3). In many cases you will have combined a transferable skill with a job skill. For example, if you identified "driver of cars and vans" as a transferable skill that you documented by car-pool driver, then the specific skill of driver can be added to your list of job skills. Or if you identified "public speaking" as one of your transferable skills, think about what your subject was. The subject of your speech—the stock market, parent-teacher relationships, or consumerism—is your job skill.

Think through all of your job skills, not just the ones you have been paid for. If you were a fund raiser for United Way or your church group, add fund raising to your list. If playing the viola in the community symphony or acting in the local playhouse was an activity of yours, add those job skills to your list, too. Get them all down on paper—in your job-hunting notebook—so that you will be able to see clearly what you can do.

STRATEGY 8

Documenting Job Skills

Again, it's necessary to document, or prove, these skills. Look at your completed job skills list and after each skill, comment or write where and how you used that skill. Be sure you can prove you have the skill and can use it now. For example, you may have studied Spanish in high school and now, 40 years later, it really isn't one of your skills. Or you may have had a year of shorthand years ago in business school and haven't used it since. Documenting your job skills list means illustrating that you have used a certain skill recently, or *could* use it with a short refresher course at an adult education program at your local high school (these courses are usually free or a nominal fee is charged) or after a short on-the-job training program.

Job or technical skills often have to be updated. Refresher courses are given in many areas for those of you who have left a particular field for a different job or for those of you who are in an ever-changing field. A six-month refresher course in nursing, for example, or a two-month typing course in adult education may be just the thing you need for your present job hunt. Check your local high school and your closest community college about refresher courses.

STRATEGY 9

Identifying Your Interests

What do you really like to do? What kinds of things make you feel good? Try to identify your interests by noticing which activities fill you with joy and which are energy producing. You can also learn what your interests are by studying the opposite feeling. Activities that drag you down, make you feel angry, depressed, bored, or that drain your energy, are activities that can tell you a lot about the kinds of jobs to keep away from.

Here is an exercise to enable you to think about your interests. In your notebook list the five activity headings below. (Use the chart on page 47 as your guide.) Now make two columns to the right of each activity, one for those you love and one for those you hate. For each activity try to list three that you love and three that you hate.

1. Home activities
2. Parenting activities
3. Learning activities
4. Work activities
5. Recreational activities

This activity will help you learn about your interests, not by what you say you like but by what you actually *do* in your daily life.

Activities	What I Love	What I Hate

Home activities
_____
_____
_____
_____

Parenting activities
_____
_____
_____
_____

Learning activities
_____
_____
_____
_____

Work activities

Recreational activities

STRATEGY 10

What Activities Do You Enjoy?

Look at the activities that make you feel good. Do you do the activities alone or with others? Notice who shares in most of the activities you love and hate. Are they people in your own age group? Are they younger or older people? Men or women? How are the activities you love related to making money? To having fun? To personal achievement? What transferable skills are involved in the activities you love? Which of your skills are needed for the activities you hate?

Another clue to your interests is time. The activities you love are those that make the time fly. When you hate an activity time drags on and on, sometimes even seeming to stand still.

Check out how you feel when you are doing the activities on your list. When are you the most "you"? When are you in a situation that brings out your best? Your worst? Work with your interest list to become more aware of yourself. No one knows more about your interests than you do. No test can measure more about you than what you already know. Trust yourself as you learn more about your interests. Notice your own behavior. The more you can define what it is you like and what it is you want, the easier it is to plan how to get it.

STRATEGY 11

Changing Interests

You can count on it. People grow. People change. And you will, too. Plan on it. If you could spend your birthday exactly the way you want, think of three activities you would choose to do—no holds barred. You could work, eat, sleep, drink, play. No "shoulds." What would you do? Write your three activity wishes in your notebook.

Next, think back five birthdays ago, and 10 and 20 birthdays ago. Let your mind drift back and remember possible activities you would have chosen to do on those birthdays. What would you have done if you could have spent those days doing anything you wanted? Would you have been alone? With anyone in particular? At work? Selling a million-dollar piece of real estate? Getting an advanced degree? Playing sports? Traveling? With your children? How was five years ago different from now? How were 20 years or 10 years ago different? Think it all out.

How about next year and five years from now? How will your life be different? How do you see your interests changing in the future? How will your job plans fit in with those changing interests? Think about those future interests; describe your top activities for a birthday three years from now.

STRATEGY 12

Clarifying Values

Now that you know more about your interests today—the things that make you feel good, the things that produce energy, that you love to do—the next strategy is to clarify your values.

Clarifying your values means deciding which interests are most important to you—what you do, where you do it, when you do it, and with whom. For instance, if you have to choose between working with someone you like on a job you aren't crazy about or alone on a job that you prefer, which would you choose? Is being with a friend or working alone more important than the activity? Is being close to home important to you, or would you turn down a better job so you wouldn't have to take a bus to work? Would you trade off your interests and take a morning job instead of a job you liked better that is offered at an inconvenient time, such as only at night? How much would you sacrifice? Would you work on Sundays? Would you work on the day you usually see your grandchildren?

You can figure out your values by looking at how you spend your time. Values are how you feel about activities and situations. These are the satisfactions you get from doing things you like. In order to be satisfied with your work you have to do what's important to you. A paycheck and good fringe benefits are satisfying, but sometimes they are not enough to enable you to be happy on the job. People often give up or trade off a satisfying job for one that is more secure. Many people aren't even aware of their trade offs and what they give up.

Take the time now to write in your job-hunting notebook three ideas or situations that are important in your life as a homemaker, worker, or club member. This might be, for example, (1) time to work alone, (2) to exercise, and (3) to make good money. Next, write down three ideas or situations that you find are a complete waste of time. Things you don't value or you find a waste of time also tell you a lot about yourself and help you to clarify your values. If you like being around people, for example, you would not like working in a job that has no interaction with others. If you can't stand committee work, you probably don't value the opinions of others. If you can't stand the city, you may value suburban or country living over any job that demands that you live in a city. Geography and lifestyle may be so important to you that you wouldn't even consider a better job that is in another town or state.

STRATEGY 13

Job Values List

Values make a difference in the kind of job you go after. When you choose a job you chose the types of people you'll work with, the amount of time you will work, and the amount of time you will have for other activities, as well as the importance of money and locality to you. When you choose a job, you choose a life situation that limits or permits growth of your particular skills and unique personality.

Here are 31 job values or satisfactions people get from their work. Read the entire list, and add some of your own.

1. Helping others
2. People contact
3. Working with others
4. Belonging to a group
5. Friendships
6. Competition
7. Making decisions
8. Working under pressure

9. Power and authority
10. Influencing people
11. Working alone
12. Knowledge
13. Intellectual status
14. Creativity
15. Aesthetics
16. Supervision
17. Change and variety
18. Precision work
19. Stability
20. Security
21. Fast pace
22. Recognition
23. Excitement
24. Adventure
25. Profit, gain
26. Independence
27. Moral fulfillment
28. Location
29. Community
30. Physical challenge
31. Time flexibility

Add your own:
32. _____
33. _____
34. _____
35. _____

STRATEGY 14

Job Values Exercise

Here is the same values list with a definition placed on each value. After you have read the value, rate each item on the list on a scale from 1 to 10, a 10 being the most valuable to you:

1. **Helping others:** Be involved in helping other people in a direct way
2. **People contact:** Have a lot of day-to-day work with people
3. **Working with others:** Have close working relationships
4. **Belonging to a group:** Be known as a member of a particular group
5. **Friendships:** Develop close personal relationships with people from work
6. **Competition:** Work in activities that pit my abilities against those of others
7. **Making decisions:** Have the power to decide action and policy at work

8. **Working under pressure:** Work in places where deadlines are common and work is critically judged by supervisors
9. **Power and authority:** Control the work activities of others
10. **Influencing people:** Be in a position to change attitudes and opinions of other people
11. **Working alone:** Do projects by myself, without much contact with others
12. **Knowledge:** Spend work time learning and understanding
13. **Intellectual status:** Be known as an "expert" in a field
14. **Creativity:** Work in art forms; create new programs
15. **Aesthetics:** Study or appreciate the beauty of things
16. **Supervision:** Be responsible for the work of others
17. **Change and variety:** Work activities that often change
18. **Precision work:** Work requirement allows no error
19. **Stability:** Work in routine job with very little change
20. **Security:** Be assured of keeping job with good pay
21. **Fast pace:** Work must be done rapidly

22. **Recognition:** Be recognized in public for work
23. **Excitement:** Experience a high degree of excitement from work
24. **Adventure:** Work includes risk taking
25. **Profit, gain:** Opportunity to make big money
26. **Independence:** Chance to be my own boss
27. **Moral fulfillment:** Work contributes to moral standards that are important to me
28. **Location:** Living near my work
29. **Community:** Live in a particular place that is more important than the work I do
30. **Physical challenge:** Physical demands that make me feel strong
31. **Time flexibility:** Able to work my own hours on my own schedule

Add your own:
32. _____
33. _____
34. _____
35. _____

Look over your list. Select those items with a score of seven or above and write them in your job-hunting notebook. Take a good look at them. What do these work values tell you about yourself? How do these values relate to each other?

What kind of work situation will bring you the greatest number of satisfactions? Discuss your job values with your family and friends. See if you can clarify your job values so that you will find a job that meets with your satisfaction, a job that will make you feel good about yourself.

STRATEGY 15

Ideal Job

You have identified your strongest transferable skills (Strategy 3), job skills (Strategy 6), interests (Strategy 9), and clarified your values (Strategy 14). It's time now for you to describe a job that involves using those skills. Think about the type of organization for which you would like to work, and decide what you would like to do there.

Look beyond the job titles such as bank teller, sales clerk, driver, small-business owner, companion. Think about a job in terms of the function—what you would actually *do* on the job. For example, an ideal job description may be "I want to work in a small company where I can perform a variety of functions, use my typing and communication skills with a chance to get to know my coworkers well. I want to work part time or share a job."

Another ideal job description may be "I want to use my outdoor interests with my lawn-, shrub-, and tree-care skills to start my own grounds-keeping business with one or two partners." Or, "I want to use my teaching and parenting skills to start a tutoring service in my home."

Write your own ideal job description in your notebook. Write another one. And one more.

STRATEGY 16

Long-range Goal Setting

Review your ideal job descriptions. Think about how each ideal job could be written into a job-hunting goal. Put a time limit on each goal—a reasonable time when you think you could be on the job. Here are some examples.

- Write the goal: Get a clerical job in a small insurance company or bank. Add a time limit: within six months.
- Write the goal: Start a grounds-keeping business. Add a time limit: within the year.
- Write the goal: Start a tutoring service. Add a time limit: within three months.

Look at your notebook. Translate your ideal job descriptions (Strategy 15) into long-range goal-setting statements. Write each one in your notebook.

STRATEGY 17

Plan of Action

What is a plan of action? It is the steps you must take to reach your long-term goal within your time limit. For example, if your long-term goal is to "start a tutoring service" with a time limit of three months, your plan of action begins with convincing your spouse that you have the time and need his or her support to achieve this long-term goal. Soon after the school year begins, make an appointment with a guidance counselor in each school in your city.

After each counselor conference, plan to follow through by sending to each counselor a description of your services, fees, and endorsements from parents of your former students. At home, convert a bedroom (that is no longer used now that the children have left home) into a study for your tutoring business.

Your plan of action, then, should include the following five steps:

1. Convince spouse of my long-term goal
2. Make appointments with guidance counselors
3. See each counselor in the city to recruit students for tutoring, in school or home
4. Follow up appointments with a mailing to each counselor
5. Convert a bedroom into a study
6. Continue to recruit students in creative ways

In your job-hunting notebook write (1) your long-term goal and (2) each step in your plan of action.

STRATEGY 18

Timetable

Make a timetable for each of the steps you are going to take in your plan of action. If three months is your time limit, get out your calendar and notebook and write each step and the actual date for each action to be completed. Keep the timetable on a separate page in your notebook where you can watch your progress. If some dates aren't met, remember that flexibility is the key to job hunting. You can revise the dates as needed. These dates are not there to disappoint you. They are to be used only as guidelines for keeping you on the job-hunting road.

Once you have a clear idea about what you can do, what you want to do, and when you want to do it, you are ready for Part II: "Where Are the Jobs?"

PART II

WHERE ARE THE JOBS?

26 Special Job-researching Strategies for Retirees

STRATEGY 19

Create a Job Possibilities List

With your skills, interests, values, and timetable in mind, the first crucial task is for you to create a job possibilities list. You will probably consider several jobs before you choose one. The job you do choose will probably come from this list. Make your job possibilities list as broad as your skills and interests permit and as narrow as is practical to consider. Where do you start?

Think first of your current job or your most recent job and your past work experiences. Are there any related jobs that have always interested you? Next, read through the list of jobs currently available in senior employment agencies (Strategy 20). Special strategies 20 through 38 are all about places or activities that will give you ideas for your job possibilities list. In your job-hunting notebook, enter at least three jobs that you might consider exploring further. Come back and add more job possibilities as you work on the next 26 strategies.

STRATEGY *20*

Senior Employment Agency Jobs

What are the jobs for retirees? What kinds of jobs have other older workers found this year? What are your options? What jobs are sitting there, waiting for you to come and take them? Here is a list of jobs waiting to be filled in senior employment agencies from Los Angeles, Houston, Chicago, Boston, San Francisco, New York, and Norwalk, Connecticut; Washington, D.C.; White Plains, New York; and Jersey City, New Jersey. These are the jobs that employers have taken to employment agencies with the specific request that they be filled by retirees and older workers.

Even in times of high unemployment, these jobs are available. The list will give you a good idea of the number of choices you have and the kinds of jobs that people from 45 to 85 are being hired to do. Most of the clients using the senior employment services are over 55, and the majority are in their 60s and 70s. The pay varies from $4 to $16.50 an hour. Most jobs are $6 an hour and can be negotiated. Here are the jobs.

ACCOUNTANT: 3 days a week, 9 A.M.–5 P.M.
ADMINISTRATIVE ASSISTANT: $11; 20 hours per week, flexible
ADMINISTRATOR, synagogue: flexible
ART SHOP OFFICE WORK: flexible
ASSISTANT BOOKKEEPER: 3 days
BABY SITTER: after school, 3–7 P.M.
BABY SITTER: $5; 2 days a week, on bus route
BANK RECEPTIONIST: 11 A.M.–3 P.M.
BANK TELLER: 11 A.M.–2 P.M.
BIOLOGY TEACHER: 1 afternoon a week
BOOKKEEPER: 3 days a week, 9 A.M.–5 P.M.
CAFETERIA WORK: 10 A.M.–2 P.M., 5 days a week
CAFETERIA WORKER: 11 A.M.–4:30 P.M.
CARPENTER: small home jobs
CASHIER: 9 A.M.–3 P.M.
CHEMIST: $12; flexible hours, 3 or 4 hours a day
CHILD CARE: in child's home, 20 to 40 hours a week
CLERICAL AID: 4 days a week
COMPANION FOR CANCER PATIENT: $5; flexible

COMPANION FOR WHEELCHAIR PATIENT: 2 days a week, 3 hours a day
COMPANION: nights only; nice home
COMPANION: $5.50; name your own hours
COMPANION: 3 days a week, 10 A.M.–3 P.M.
COOK: 3 days a week, 4–7 P.M.
COUNSELOR: 3 afternoons a week
COURIER: $6; 4 hours per day
CRAFTS TEACHER: Scouts on Thursdays, 1:30–3:30 P.M.
DRAFTSMAN: 4 mornings a week
DRAFTSMAN: flexible hours
DRIVER: 2 days a week
DRIVER: $4.50; 9 A.M.–1:30 P.M.
DRIVER: $7; 3 hours a day
ENGINEER *chemical processing:* part time
EXECUTIVE SEARCH: at home
FOOD HANDLER: 5 days a week, 9 A.M.–9 P.M.
GARDENER: 4 hours a day, April to September
GENERAL OFFICE WORK: 2 days a week
GUY OR GAL FRIDAY: flexible time
HAIR STUDIO: $5; errands, odd jobs; weekends
HORTICULTURE TEACHER: 4 days a week
HOSPITAL AID: flexible
INSTRUCTORS: 8:30 A.M.–2 P.M.
INVENTORY TAKING: part time; permanent
LIBRARY AID: 3–5 P.M., 3 days a week
LIFE INSURANCE SALES: will train, 10 A.M.–3 P.M., five days a week

MAIL-ROOM ASSISTANT: $6.30; afternoons, 21 hours a week
MAIL-ROOM CLERK: 2 months
MAINTENANCE PERSON: $5; 5 mornings a week
MEDICAL TECHNOLOGIST: flexible
MESSENGER: mornings
MESSENGER: $4; 8 A.M. to noon
PAID NEIGHBOR: flexible time
PHARMACY CLERK: $5.50; 6 mornings a week
PHOTOGRAPHY SHOP: 2 evenings a week
QUALITY CONTROL PERSON IN PRINTING: half time
READER: financial section of daily papers, $6; 2 afternoons a week
RECEPTIONIST: $6; 10 A.M.–3:30, Monday through Friday
RECEPTIONIST: 1 day a week
RECEPTIONIST: no typing, $6; 8:30 A.M.–12:30 P.M.
RECEPTIONIST: 9 A.M.–1 P.M.
SALES CLERK: 11 A.M.–3 P.M.
SALES CLERK: 2 months
SECURITY GUARD: share a job, 20 hours a week
SECURITY GUARDS: $4; weekends
SECURITY GUARD: 4:30 P.M. to 9 P.M.
SENIOR'S COMPANION: 3 afternoons a week
SEWING MACHINE OPERATOR: 20 hours a week

SHIPPING CLERK: 5 mornings a week
SWITCHBOARD: noon to 5 P.M.
TEACHER: $15; flexible time, must have car
TEACHER'S AID: 4 hours a day
TELEMARKETING (telephone sales): up to $9 per hour; 3 shifts available
TELEPHONE OUTREACH: $6; 3 to 5 evenings a week
TENNIS-COURT ATTENDANT: 9 A.M.–4 P.M., 3 days a week
TRAINING CONSULTANT: $20,000 a year; 4 months a year
TRAVEL REPRESENTATIVE: flexible
TV SECRETARY: 9 A.M.–5 P.M., 2 or 3 days per week
TYPE LETTERS: 1 month
TYPIST: $6; 9 A.M.–3 P.M., 2 days a week
WORD PROCESSOR: $16.50; pick your own time

STRATEGY 21

Senior Agency's Easiest Jobs to Fill

"The easiest jobs I have to fill are for skilled typists, accountants, bookkeepers, receptionists, and secretaries." This is a statement often made by senior employment counselors. "These jobs come in all the time, there is a big turnover, and we fill them easily. People who have a particular skill can name their own hours and days. Office jobs are in demand, and anyone who wants one can easily find one."

"Retail sales on a part-time basis are easy to fill. Most department stores want part-time help, and many retirees have friends who are in retail stores. They don't feel out of place and have other older people they enjoy working with."

"Companion jobs are usually easy to fill. If the family is right and it's a nice home, many retirees are happy being a companion. We get a lot of requests for companion jobs—some people need more care than others; some are for practical nurses—but mostly just someone around to cook and drive and visit with." Most companion jobs are part-time jobs, although there are a lot of seasonal companion jobs.

One small Vermont community has a network of companion jobs in Florida, in the Sarasota area. One friend gets another a job, mostly people in their 70s serving others in their 80s. They go for six winter months a year, get their flight paid from Vermont, get their room and board and earn between $100 and $200 a week. The Vermonters get together for holidays and bring their companions with them. Besides making money, the companions save Vermont fuel bills and all of their Social Security checks. The job adds a good $5,000 a year toward making ends meet. In summer, the Vermont companions return to their big homes and live like older people are "expected" to live when they are in their 70s—"retired."

Any skilled trade such as carpenter, plumber, electrician can be easily filled. The same is true for nurses, computer technicians, machinists, welders, or word-processor operators. If you have a skill, age is no factor in getting a job.

STRATEGY 22

Senior Agency's Hardest Jobs to Fill

"I can't fill commission sales jobs—older people won't touch them," says a senior employment counselor. Another agency volunteer said, "Older people want to know how much money they are going to get for the hours they put in. They don't want to take a chance on commission sales."

"I can't fill baby-sitting and child-care jobs—they come in every day. Older people have 'had it' with child care. They don't want the responsibilities and the commotion and low pay that goes with it." Child care is the biggest *unfilled* job area.

Liquor stores and motels are two sites in which job openings can't be filled. "They are too dangerous. You read about hold-ups all the time at these places."

Outdoor jobs are also hard to fill. "I can't fill outside jobs either—no one will take them."

"Many people come in and say they desperately want a job, they need the money and want something to do for 15 or 20 hours a week. They say they will take anything. But they don't mean *anything*. They won't take any of these jobs we can't fill!"

"Bank teller jobs are still another job area that often opens up, but our clients say they won't take them. They have to be on their feet all day, and the salaries are low for the amount of responsibility and pressure."

If you really are desperate for a job, look to an agency or put an ad in your local paper for any of the preceding jobs that are "impossible to fill."

STRATEGY 23

Largest Number of New Jobs

It will help to know what the largest number of new jobs will be. Here is the latest outlook from the U.S. Department of Labor, a list starting with the job predicted to have biggest growth in numbers of new jobs predicted until 1995.

Cashiers
Registered nurses
Janitors and cleaners, including housekeeping
Truck drivers
Waiters and waitresses
Wholesale trade salesworkers
Nursing aides, orderlies, attendants
Salespersons
Accountants and auditors
Teachers, elementary and kindergarten
Secretaries

Computer programmers
General office clerks
Food preparation workers
Computer systems analysts
Electrical and electronic engineers
Electrical and electronic technicians
Guards
Automotive and motorcycle mechanics
Lawyers
Cosmetologists
Cooks
Maintenance repairers
Bookkeepers
Bartenders
Computer operators
Licensed practical nurses
Carpenters
Switchboard operators
Food service and lodging managers
Electricians
Teacher aides and educational assistants
Blue-collar worker supervisors
Receptionists and information clerks
Mechanical engineers

STRATEGY 24

Where Are the Jobs?

Do you wonder where the best chances for work are? Are you thinking of moving to a warmer climate and wondering if the job opportunities are as good there as they are where you live? Economists say that these cities offer the best chances for work and are the least expensive to live in.

Arizona
Phoenix
Tuscon

Florida
Fort Lauderdale
Hollywood Beach
Tampa

California
San Diego

New Mexico
Alburquerque

Colorado
Denver
Boulder

Oklahoma
Tulsa

The regions that provide the best chances for jobs follow.

West Coast: California, Nevada, Arizona, and Hawaii are booming with defense contracts, creating technical, clerical, and service jobs at all levels of employment.

Southeast: Florida, especially around Tampa, has very good job opportunities, especially for skilled workers.

Mountain States, New England, Middle Atlantic States, and the Midwest have very high unemployment. The fewest chances for work are in the Midwest, especially in Michigan, Illinois, and Ohio, and also in upstate New York.

Keep in mind that if you live in a part of the country where job opportunities are poor it doesn't mean that there are no jobs, nor that you won't ever get one. It does mean that it's harder to get a job. You may need to take more time, use more resources, and accept a job that is not quite as good as you had hoped to get. Be flexible, and brush up your job skills. These are the keys to winning a job—no matter what region of the country you live in.

STRATEGY 25

Companies with Special Programs for Older Workers

The companies noted here have special programs for retirees and older workers such as part-time work, job sharing, phased retirement, sabbatical leaves, time-income trade offs, reduction in work hours, shorter work weeks, and extended holidays and leaves.

If you work for a company that doesn't have special programs such as job-sharing or phased retirement, you can show your personnel officer this impressive list. Suggest that the company work out a plan for *you* and other older workers by using the list as a model example of your plan.

Many of the companies on the list have branch offices all over the United States. The state the company is listed under is often the site of the company's headquarters or the largest employer. In some cases, there are branches in many regions of a particular state. You needn't have worked for any of these companies in the past to qualify as an older worker on a special program. Check out every company and employment opportunity whether you have ever worked there before or not. And be sure to show your own company this list. Maybe they'll start a special program of their own, if they haven't yet.

ARIZONA
Bullock's Department Stores
Western Savings & Loan Association, Sun City

CALIFORNIA
Atlantic Richfield Company, Los Angeles
Duncan Enterprises, Fresno
Flexible Career Associates, Santa Barbara
Hastings College of the Law
Hewlett-Packard, Palo Alto
Kaiser Cement, Oakland
Levi Strauss and Company, San Francisco
Lockhead Corporation, Burbank
Mary Jane Company, North Hollywood
Northrop Corporation, Anaheim
ROLM Corporation, Santa Clara
San Francisco Unified School District

TRW Vidar, Sunnyvale
United California Bank, Southern California
Varian Associates, Palo Alto
Vendo Company, Pinedale
Wells Fargo and Company, San Francisco

CONNECTICUT
Aetna Life and Casualty, Hartford
American Can Company, Greenwich
American Velvet, Stonington
Connecticut General Life Insurance Company
Connecticut Mutual Life Insurance Company, Hartford
Conoco Inc., Stamford
Fertl, Inc., Norwalk
General Electric, Fairfield
The International Silver Company, Meriden
Travelers Insurance Companies, Hartford
Xerox Corporation, Stamford

DELAWARE
E. I. du Pont de Nemours & Company, Wilmington

DISTRICT OF COLUMBIA
American Council of Life Insurance, Washington
Lieb, Lefkowitz Associates, Washington
McManis & Associates, Washington
Woodward & Lothrop Department Stores

GEORGIA
Atlanta Part-time Professionals, Atlanta

ILLINOIS
Bankers Life and Casualty Company, Chicago
Borg-Warner Corporation, Chicago
Harris Trust and Savings Bank, Chicago
Illinois Bell Telephone Company
McDonald's Corporation, Oak Brook
Motorola, Schaumburg
Sunstrand Corporation, Rockford
Swift & Company, Chicago
The Wrigley Company, Chicago

MARYLAND
The Black and Decker Manufacturing Company, Towson
Maryland State Automobile Insurance Fund

MASSACHUSETTS
First National Bank of Boston
New England Mutual Life Insurance Company, Boston
Polaroid Corporation, Cambridge
Towle Silversmiths, Inc., Newburyport

MICHIGAN
Ford Motor Company, Detroit
General Motors, Detroit

Tomkins-Johnson Division, Aeroquip
   Corporation, Jackson
United Steel Workers of America, Detroit

MINNESOTA
Control Data Corporation, Minneapolis
Honeywell, Minneapolis
The Toro Company, Bloomington
Medtronic, Inc., Minneapolis

NEBRASKA
Mutual of Omaha, Omaha
Northern Natural Gas Company, Omaha

NEW JERSEY
Bell Laboratories, Short Hills
BMW of North America, Montvale
Merck & Company, Rahway

NEW YORK
Amalgamated Clothing & Textiles Workers,
   New York City
American Express Company, New York City
Associated Dry Goods, New York City
Chase Manhattan Bank, New York City
Citibank, New York City
Corning Glass Works, Houghton Park
Equitable Life Assurance, New York City
Grumman Aerospace, Bethpage

IBM, Armonk
J. C. Penney, New York City
Macy's, New York City
Metropolitan Life Insurance, New York City
Morgan Guaranty Trust Company,
  New York City
New York Life, New York City
Pfizer, Inc., New York City
Philip Morris, Inc., New York City
RCA Corporation, New York City
Towers, Perrin, Forster & Crosby, New York
  City

NORTH CAROLINA
Fieldcrest Mills, Eden

OHIO
Firestone Tire Company, Akron
The Mead Corporation, Dayton
Sherwin Williams, Cleveland

OREGON
Evans Products, Portland

PENNSYLVANIA
Mack Trucks, Allentown
Pennsylvania Power & Light Company,
  Allentown
Sun Company, Radnor

TEXAS
American Airlines, Dallas
Exxon, Houston
Shell Oil Company, Houston
Southwestern Life Insurance, Dallas

UTAH
Phoenix Institute, Salt Lake City

WISCONSIN
Johnson Wax, Racine
Northwestern Mutual Life Insurance, Milwaukee
Oscar Mayer, Madison

STRATEGY 26

State Office on the Aging

The first place to look for help in getting a job is your own state office on the aging. This office is set up by your governor and your state legislature to help older persons, whatever their needs. If your need is employment, your state office is listed here. Many states have special sections organized exclusively for senior employment. Other state agencies will tell you where you can find information on senior employment. Still others will refer you to your area agency on aging. Ask them for advice on what you should do next and who in your state government will help you. Every state is required by law to be divided into area agencies on the aging.

Some state offices will have a job bank of their own or will know of new senior agencies that are available in your area. This up-to-date list kept by your state agency may offer some good ideas for your next employment move.

ALABAMA
Emmett Eaton, Executive Director
　Commission on Aging
Montgomery, AL 36130
(205) 261-5743

ALASKA
Jon Wolfe, Executive Director
　Older Alaskans Commission
Pouch C–Mail Station 2909, Juneau, AK 99811
(907) 465-3250

ARIZONA
Michael Slattery, Director
　Aging and Adult Administration
1400 West Washington Street, Phoenix,
　AZ 85007
(602) 255-4446

ARKANSAS
Herb Sanderson, Director
　Office of Aging and Adult Services
Donaghey Building, Suite 1428, 7th and Main

Streets, Little Rock, AR 72201
(501) 371-2442

CALIFORNIA
Alice Gonzales, Director, Department of Aging
1020 19th Street, Sacramento, CA 95814
(916) 322-5290

COLORADO
William Hanna, Director, Aging and Adult
 Services Division, Department of Social
 Services
1573 Sherman Street, Room 503, Denver,
 CO 80203
(303) 866-3672

CONNECTICUT
Mary Ellen Klinck, Executive Director,
 Department on Aging
175 Main Street, Hartford, CT 06106
(203) 566-3238

DELAWARE
Eleanor Cain, Director, Division on Aging
1901 North DuPont Highway, New Castle,
 DE 19720
(302) 421-6791

DISTRICT OF COLUMBIA
Veronica Pace, Executive Director, Office on Aging
1424 K Street, NW, 2nd Floor, Washington DC 20011
(202) 724-5626

FLORIDA
Margaret Lynn Duggar, Director, Program Office of Aging and Adult Services
1317 Winewood Blvd., Tallahassee, FL 32301
(904) 488-8922

GEORGIA
Fred McGinnis, Director, Office of Aging
878 Peachtree Street, N.E., Room 632, Atlanta, GA 30309
(404) 894-5333

HAWAII
Renji Goto, Director, Executive Office on Aging, Office of the Governor
1149 Bethel Street, Room 307, Honolulu, Hawaii 96813
(808) 548-2593

ILLINOIS
Janet S. Otwell, Director, Department on Aging

421 East Capitol Avenue, Springfield, IL 62701
(217) 785-2870

INDIANA
Jean Merritt, Executive Director, Department of
  Aging and Community Services
115 North Pennsylvania Street, Suite 1350,
  Consolidated Building, Indianapolis, IN 46204
(317) 232-7006

IOWA
Karen Tynes, Executive Director, Commission
  on Aging
Suite 236, Jewett Building, 914 Grand Avenue,
  Des Moines, IA 50319
(515) 281-5187

KANSAS
Joyce V. Romero, Secretary, Department on
  Aging
610 West Tenth, Topeka, KS 66612
(913) 296-4986

KENTUCKY
Marge Brock, Director, Division for Aging
  Services, Department of Human Resources
DHR Building, 6th Floor, 275 Main Street,
  Frankfort, KY 40601
(502) 564-6930

LOUISIANA
Sandra Adams, Director, Office of Elderly Affairs
P.O. Box 80374, Baton Rouge, LA 70898
(504) 925-1700

MAINE
Patricia Riley, Director, Bureau of Maine's
  Elderly Department of Human Services
Station #11, Augusta, ME 04333
(207) 289-2561

MARYLAND
Rosalie Abrams, Director, Office on Aging
State Office Building, 301 West Preston Street,
  Room 1004, Baltimore, MD 21201
(301) 225-1100

MASSACHUSETTS
Richard Rowland, Director, Department of
  Elderly Affairs
38 Chauncy Street, Boston, MA 02111
(617) 727-7750

MICHIGAN
Olivia Maynard, Director, Office of Services to
  the Aging
P.O. Box 30026, Lansing, MI 48909
(517) 373-8230

MINNESOTA
Gerald Bledow, Executive Director, Board on Aging
Metro Square Building, Room 204, Seventh and Robert Streets, St. Paul, MN 55101
(612) 296-2544

MISSISSIPPI
David K. Brown, Director, Council on Aging
301 West Pearl Street, Jackson, MS 39203-3092
(601) 949-2070

MISSOURI
Lloyd Conley, Director, Division on Aging, Department of Social Services
Broadway State Office, P.O. Box 570, Jefferson City, MO 65101
(314) 751-3082

MONTANA
Norma Harris, Administrator, Community Services Division
P.O. Box 4210, Helena, MT 59604
(406) 444-3865

NEBRASKA
Helen Boosalis, Director, Department of Aging
P.O. Box 95044, 301 Centennial Mall, South Lincoln, NE 68509
(402) 471-2306

NEVADA
Myla Florence, Executive Director, Division on Aging
505 East King Street, Kinkead Building, Room 101, Carson City, NV 89710
(702) 885-4210

NEW HAMPSHIRE
Anna M. Pluhar, Director, Council on Aging
14 Depot Street, Concord, NH 03301
(603) 271-2751

NEW JERSEY
Ann Zahora, Director, Division on Aging
P.O. Box 2768, Trenton, NJ 08625
(609) 292-4833

NEW MEXICO
Rita Maes, Director, State Agency on Aging
224 East Palace Avenue, 4th Floor, La Villa Rivera Building, Santa Fe, NM 87501
(505) 827-7640

NEW YORK
Eugene Callender, Director, Office for the Aging
New York State Plaza Agency Building #2, Albany, NY 12223
(518) 474-4425

NORTH CAROLINA
Elaine Stoops, Assistant Secretary, Division on Aging
708 Hillsborough Street, Suite 200, Raleigh, NC 27603
(919) 733-3983

NORTH DAKOTA
Larry Brewster, Administrator, Aging Services
State Capitol Building, Bismarck, ND 58505
(701) 224-2577

OHIO
Joyce Chapple, Executive Director, Department on Aging
50 West Broad Street, 9th Floor, Columbia, OH 43215
(614) 466-5500

OKLAHOMA
Roy Keen, Supervisor, Special Unit on Aging
P.O. Box 25352, Oklahoma City, OK 73125
(405) 521-2281

OREGON
Richard Ladd, Administrator, Senior Services Division
313 Public Services Building, Salem, OR 97310
(503) 378-4728

PENNSYLVANIA
Alma Jacobas, Secretary, Department of Aging
231 State Street, Harrisburg, PA 17101–1195
(717) 783-1550

RHODE ISLAND
Adelaide Luber, Director, Department of Elderly Affairs
79 Washington Street, Providence, RI 02903
(401) 277-2858

SOUTH CAROLINA
Harry Bryan, Executive Director, Commission on Aging
915 Main Street, Columbia, SC 29201
(803) 758-2576

SOUTH DAKOTA
Michael Vogel, Executive Director, Office of Adult Services and Aging
700 North Illinois Street, Pierre, SD 57501
(605) 773-3656

TENNESSEE
Emily Wiseman, Executive Director, Commission on Aging
715 Tennessee Building, 535 Church Street, Nashville, TN 37219
(615) 741-2056

TEXAS
Bob Bobbitt, Director, Department on Aging
1949 IH 35 South, 3rd Floor, P.O. Box 12786
  Capitol Station, Austin, TX 78704
(512) 444-2727

UTAH
Robert K. Ward, Director, Division of Aging and
  Adult Services
150 West North Temple, Box 2500, Salt Lake
  City, UT 84102
(801) 533-6422

VERMONT
Joel Cook, Director, Office on Aging
102 South Main Street, Waterbury, VT 05676
(802) 241-2400

VIRGINIA
Wilda Ferguson, Commissioner, Department on
  Aging
101 North 14th Street, 18th Floor, Richmond,
  VA 23219
(804) 225-2271

WASHINGTON
Charles Reed, Director, Bureau of Aging and
  Adult Services
OB–43G, Olympia, WA 98504
(206) 753-2502

WEST VIRGINIA
Phil Turner, Director, Commission on Aging
Holly Grove-State Capitol, Charleston,
 WV 25305
(304) 348-3317

WISCONSIN
Donna McDowell, Director, Bureau of Aging
One West Wilson Street, Room 480, Madison,
 WI 53702
(608) 266-2536

WYOMING
Scott Sessions, Director, Commission on Aging
Hathaway Building, Room 139, Cheyenne,
 WY 82002–0710
(307) 777-7986

GUAM
Franklin Cruz, Director, Public Health and
 Social Services, Government of Guam
Agana, Guam 96910

PUERTO RICO
Pura Quesada Pico, Executive Director,
 Gericulture Commission
P.O. Box 11398, Santurce, Puerto Rico 00910
(809) 724-7400

STRATEGY 27

State Job Service

You will find the phone number and address of your state job service in the white pages of your telephone book under the state listing of the Employment Security Department. Check with them for a list of jobs, looking especially for those on your job possibility list (Strategy 19). If you learn of any other jobs that use your particular skills, add them to your job list in your job-hunting notebook.

Unless your state job service has an older-worker specialist you will probably find that you won't get much help. Since people over 70 are not covered by the federal age discrimination in employment act, older people do not legally have to be a priority for job placement. Most older people get more discouragement than encouragement from their state employment service! But you can still use the service for a list of possible job ideas available in your area. And who knows? Maybe you'll be lucky and there will happen to be someone there who talks to older grown-ups!

STRATEGY 28

Private Employment Agencies

Unless they advertise for older workers (senior, 55+, 40+, mature, or retired workers), you probably won't get much help from private employment agencies. In fact, many of them will refuse to accept applications from anyone over 55. No job hunter needs discouraging encounters in his or her search. Go to an agency that includes older workers in its mission, or better yet, reaches out for them.

STRATEGY 29

Private Employment Service for Older Workers

TempsAmerica started out as Mature Temps, the biggest and best known special employment service for older workers. It was so successful "selling" older workers to corporate business, that it had to expand to servicing workers of all ages to get the numbers of business office workers needed for the demand. TempsAmerica will test you, interview you, and evaluate you. It will hire and pay employees directly. The agency is paid directly by the company for which its employees are working. Most of the thousands of jobs it fills each year in all parts of the country are clerical and secretarial. These jobs are not permanent; "temps" fill in for regular salaried employees or help out on special projects. Wages range from

$7.50 to $9.00 an hour for a clerical or receptionist's job to $16.50+ for a word-processing job.

Here is a job description list that can help you see the different levels of each business office position that best fits your skills. TempsAmerica uses this classification to decide who can do what and also to decide how much money you will get. You can look for a job *without* TempsAmerica to help you. This classification for business office jobs will be the same everywhere. Use the rates of pay as a guideline to know what you should expect to get paid, in a similar job that you find on your own.

ACCOUNTING CLERKS
H13.0. *Accounts Payable Clerk:* $9.00 to $9.75
Prepares all disbursement items for payment. May prepare bank reconciliations. Handles all incoming and outgoing accounts payable mail. May manually prepare checks. Capable of operating 10-key adding machine and calculator.

H14.0. *Accounts Receivable Clerk:* Open pay
Has basic bookkeeping knowledge. Checks, posts, and reconciles accounts receivable ledgers or journals. Processes invoices for payment. Performs intermediate calculations such as percentages. Operates an adding machine or calculator.

H11.0. *Payroll Clerk:* $9.00 to $9.75
Computes payroll from time cards. Prepares reports, quarterly summaries, compiles checks and W-2 forms. May do some typing and clerical functions. Capable of operating a 10-key adding machine or calculator.

BOOKKEEPERS
H15.0. *Assistant Bookkeeper:* $9.00 to $9.75
Full knowledge of bookkeeping procedures through trial balance. Maintains books of general accounts under supervision. May be responsible for supervising accounts payable and accounts receivable clerks and preparation of checks. Operates 10-key adding machine as well as other accounting machines.

H16.0. *Full-Charge Bookkeeper:*
   Professional—Open
Has a minimum of three years' experience and an extensive knowledge of bookkeeping procedures. Maintains books for general accounting. Prepares all worksheets for balancing books. Capable of preparing profit-and-loss statements, trial balances, and cost-accounting reports. Operates accounting machines.

CLERKS
A18.0. *Figure Clerk:* $7.50 to $9.00

Has good math ability. Compiles numerical data from specific sources for statistical reports. May be asked to prepare computation based on standardized formulas under supervision. May be asked to post data on charts and graphs and to prepare statistical reports in final copy. Capable of using 10-key adding machine or calculator.

A13.1. *File Clerk:* $7.50 to $9.00
Codes, sorts, and files unclassified material using an alphabetical, numerical, or chronological system. Indexes and cross references materials. May be asked to perform related tasks such as preparing handwritten forms and cross checking information.

A13.2. *General Office Clerk:* $7.50 to $9.00
Can perform overall clerical functions, which may include filing, light typing, or handwriting of forms, labels, or envelopes. May also serve as back-up support for accounting clerks, receptionists, typists, or mail-room clerk.

C11.1. *Receptionist:* $7.50 to $9.00
Has good appearance and good speaking voice. Receives, directs, and screens visitors. Operates call directory. Maintains log of calls and visitors. May be asked to perform light typing and clerical duties such as handwriting lists, envelopes, cards, and labels.

WORD PROCESSING SERVICES

B47.0. *Word Processor:* $16.50 and up
Types 50 to 60 WPM. Is familiar with one or more types of word-processing equipment. Types correspondence, reports, proposals, and manuscripts on word-processing equipment. May be requested to set up drafts, work from previously stored materials, and edit or revise format. Has good grammar, punctuation, and spelling abilities and a good understanding of business procedures.

IBM Display Writer
Xerox 860
Lanier
Wang
Vydec
QYX
Micom

DATA PROCESSING

D11.0. *CRT Data Entry Typist:* $9.00 to $9.75
Using a keyboard, types in information to an on-line computer. Types 50 WPM.

D15.2. *Data Control Clerk:* Open
Assists in the maintenance of records to control and verify the accuracy of input and output for a data-processing system. Performs distribution of data-processing reports and other output.

D11.1 *Key Punch Operator:* $9.00 to $9.75
Under supervision, enters data via a keyboard using either an alphabetical or numeric code. Using systematic instructions, may be required to produce programming cards. May also be able to operate a card verifier.

Secretaries

G24.0. *Executive Secretary:* $12.75 to $14.25
Has excellent communication skills, good organizational ability. Takes dictation at 80 to 120 WPM. Types 60 to 70 WPM. May be required to handle confidential information and to set up schedules, appointments, meetings, and travel arrangements.

G23.0. *General Secretary:* $12.00 to $13.50
Works for one or more people with minimal supervision. Types 50 to 60 WPM. May either take dictation at 70 to 80 WPM or operate transcription equipment. May originate own correspondence under supervision.

B38.2. *Transcriber:* $10.50 to $11.25
Operates transcription equipment. Types 50 WPM. Has good grammar and spelling abilities.

These rates are all for *temporary* a-day-at-a-time jobs. Remember that clerical and secretarial jobs are easiest to get. There is a constant demand for skilled office workers everywhere in the country.

Richard Ross, president of TempsAmerica, has worked with older workers of varied job experience and employers who are looking to hire mature workers. Through his experience, he believes in the value of experience. He knows that older workers are an asset in business. He proves over and over again to insurance companies, banks, legal firms, finance organizations, manufacturers, people in medicine, electronics companies, educators, publishers and many more that it pays to hire mature people. As Ross says, "We don't talk about the age of the workers we are trying to place. We talk in terms of experience and productivity." You can do the same thing in your résumé and interview. Here is a list of cities where TempsAmerica has an office. If there isn't one in your locality, know that the same kinds of office jobs are in demand everywhere in the country. You can evaluate your own skills. You can call several companies and ask to be put on their substitute list. You can use the foregoing rates as your guideline. After you've had some experience, negotiate for more. You're worth it!

CALIFORNIA
Downey: (212) 861-7873
Irvine: (714) 476-5060
Los Angeles: 3660 Wilshire Blvd.
        (213) 380-6830

3550 Wilshire Blvd.
(213) 380-6515
Avenue of the Stars
(213) 277-3194
Pasadena: South Lake Avenue
(818) 796-1363
San Francisco: (415) 986-7787
Walnut Creek: (415) 932-5424

NEW YORK
New York City: 42nd Street
(212) 286-0180
Wall Street
(212) 732-3408

PENNSYLVANIA
Philadelphia: (215) 665-1154
Plymouth Meeting: (215) 825-4400

TEXAS
Carrollton: (214) 245-0784
Dallas: 350 N. St. Paul Street
(214) 922-9229
14114 Dallas Parkway
(214) 385-8176
Irving: (214) 556-1923

STRATEGY 30

Operation ABLE

If Chicago, Boston, Los Angeles, or San Francisco is where you live and you're over 55 and looking for a job, you're lucky! That's where you'll find Operation ABLE, the "Good Work Knows No Age" service that creates employment opportunities for older workers. Even columnist Ann Landers spreads the word about ABLE. Even if you don't live in the Chicago area, you can still learn some valuable strategies in your own area from ABLE's experience there. Shirley Brussell, the executive director of ABLE, is teaching other agencies about employment for older workers and is known throughout the country for her pioneer work, which provides

- Job clubs
- Job-hunting skills workshops
- Résumé writing
- Interview techniques
- Job leads

With its Chicago-based network of 46 special employment agencies for older workers, ABLE placed 5,000 applicants in one year. Call the ABLE Job Hotline that will put you in touch with the best Chicago location for you—(312) 782-7700.

With the same special attention to older workers, here are three more agencies with the ABLE mission:

Operation ABLE of Greater Boston
West Trade Center, Commonwealth Pier, Boston, MA 02210-2004
Contact: Gwen Harper (617) 338-0213

California ABLE
870 Market Street, San Francisco, CA 94102
Contact: John Scanlon (415) 319-5030

Los Angeles Council on Careers for Older Americans
5514 Wilshire Blvd., Suite 401, Los Angeles, CA 90036
Contact: Ann Ransford (213) 939-0391

STRATEGY 31

Urban League

SENIORS IN COMMUNITY SERVICE

If you're 55 or over and considered to be in a low-income bracket, you may qualify for an Urban League federally-funded training and employment program. This program prepares you to be job-ready for positions in the public and private sector. Look in the white pages of your telephone book under "Urban League." Thousands of retirees all over the United States get jobs through Urban League. While in the program you will receive free medical checkups, free education, free employment evaluation, free counseling, free job-search workshops, and best of all, placement in a community-service job such as teacher aide, library aide, hospital aide, or clerical aide in non-profit agencies and centers.

Most people with the Urban League program work 25 hours a week at minimum wage, averaging 1,300 hours a year and earning just over $4,000 a year.

If you haven't any other place to turn, call your Urban League, regardless of your income. In many communities, the Urban League will help you with questions about employment, even though you may not qualify for their program.

STRATEGY 32

Nonprofit Employment Agencies for Older Workers

You would think that if everyone were so interested in helping retirees get jobs there would be one list of special employment agencies for retirees and older workers. But there isn't! The closest thing to a master list is the following directory of the National Association of Older Worker Employment Services, 1984. These agencies are members of the National Council on Aging. Even though each state isn't represented on this list, this is the best information available: a state-by-state list of special agencies just for you. If there is one listed in your area, that's the best place to start your job search. Take your ideal job (Strategy

15) and your job possibilities list (Strategy 19) with you and add to it. Use your list for discussion of other potential jobs. The agency will have job-hunting counseling, workshops, placement, and personnel who will be eager to help you find a job!

ALABAMA
EDGE Employment Service, Focus on Senior
 Citizens
2902 6th Street, Tuscaloosa, AL 36401
Contact: Mary R. Graham (205) 758-3393 (55+,
 Tuscaloosa County)

ARIZONA
Coconino County Community Services
113 W. Clay, Flagstaff, AZ 86001
Contact: Joe C. Montoya, Director
 (602) 779-6753 (Coconino County)

Human Resources Department, City of Phoenix
320 West Washington, Phoenix, AZ 85003

CALIFORNIA
Los Angeles Council on Careers for Older
 Americans
5514 Wilshire Blvd., Suite 401, Los Angeles,
 CA 90036
Contact: Carol Cronin (213) 939-0391

138 • MAKING MORE MONEY

The National Council on the Aging, Senior
   Community Service Project,
650 South Spring Street, Room 719, Los
   Angeles, CA 90014
Contact: Natalie Gold, Project Manager
   (213) 622-6151 (55+)

Senior Citizens' Services, City of San Diego
202 C Street, San Diego, CA 92101
Contact: Evelyn S. Herrmann (619) 236-5765
   (45+)

S.O.S.
1150 Tenth Street, Suite 114, Long Beach,
   CA 90813
Contact: Harry S. Kilgo (213) 435-7511, ext. 291

COLORADO
AARP
2340 Robinson Street, Suite 212 (P.O. Box
   6387), Colorado Springs, CO 80934
Contact: (303) 635-3579 (55+)

City of Boulder, Senior Services
909 Aprapahoe Avenue, Boulder, CO 80302
Contact: Cay Graca (303) 441-3148 (55+,
   Boulder County)

CONNECTICUT
Sage Advocate Employment Service

248 Orange Street, New Haven, CT 06510
Contact: Natalie M. Radding (203) 777-7401
   (55+)

West Hartford Seniors Job Bank
50 South Main Street, West Hartford, CT 06107
Contact: Patricia L. Newton (203) 521-3210
   (55+)

DELAWARE
Wilmington Senior Center
1901 Market Street, Wilmington, DE 19802
Contact: Bruce Livingston (302) 651-3440

FLORIDA
Jewish Vocational Service
318 N.W. 25th Street, Miami, FL 33128
Contact: Sandra James (305) 576-3220

GEORGIA
Golden Age Employment Service
34 Tenth Street, N.W., Atlanta, GA 30309
Contact: Betty E. Jacobi, Director
   (404) 881-3982

Decatur office:
140 E. Ponce de Leon Avenue, Decatur,
   GA 30030
Contact: (404) 377-0428

ILLINOIS

Chicago Lighthouse for the Blind
1850 W. Roosevelt Road, Chicago, IL 60608
Contact: Diane Rhein (312) 666-1331 (if blind and over 55)

Illinois Department on Aging
421 E. Capitol, Springfield, IL 62703
Contact: Harriet R. Howell (217) 785-2870

Operation ABLE
36 South Wabash Avenue, Suite 714, Chicago, IL 60603
Contact: (312) 782-3335 (See Strategy 30, page 132)

INDIANA

Fort Wayne Urban League Seniors in Community Service
1205 E. Lewis, Fort Wayne, IN 48603
Contact: Michelle Gillam (219) 424-6326

Senior Enterprises
2 West Vermont, Indianapolis, IN 46204
Contact: Marcia Levin (317) 634-7007

KANSAS

Senior Services
335 W. Lewis, Wichita, KS 67202
Contact: Claire Porams (316) 267-0302

LOUISIANA
East Baton Rouge Council on Aging—Senior Employment
1628 Florida Street, Baton Rouge, LA 70802
Contact: Sara Sims (504) 926-4732

MAINE
Western Older Citizens Council
65 Central Avenue; P.O. Box 659, Lewiston, ME 04240
Contact: Robert Armstrong (207) 784-8797

MARYLAND
Associated Placement and Guidance Bureau
5750 Park Heights Avenue, Baltimore, MD 21215
Contact: Donna Krause, Director (301) 466-9200

Over-60 Employment Counseling Service of Maryland
309 N. Charles Street, Baltimore MD 21201
Contact: John Dallam (301) 752-7876

MICHIGAN
Area Agencies on Aging Associations of Michigan
Plaza Center, 111 South Capitol Avenue, Lansing, MI 48902
Contact: July Hollister (517) 482-4871

Clinton Senior Center
40700 Romeo Plank Road, Mt. Clemens,
 MI 48044
Contact: Jacqueline Kwiatek, Director
 (313) 286-8000, ext. 307

Hazlett Outreach Program
6545 Hazlett, Detroit, MI 47210
Contact: Bertha L. Chastang (313) 896-8425
 (55 +, low income)

MISSOURI
County Older Resident Program
855 S. Brentwood Blvd., Clayton, MO 63105
Contact: Jane Vickray (314) 962-7999 (employs
 60 +, previous CETA)

Jewish Vocational Services
1608 Baltimore, Kansas City, MO 64108
Contact: Stanley B. Lavine (816) 471-2808 (55 +)

Senior Community Service Project
2008 Sergeant, Room 405, Joplin, MO 64801
Contact: Jessie Patterson (417) 781-7562 (55 +,
 SW MO)

NEBRASKA
Lincoln Area Agency on Aging
901 P Street, Lincoln, NE 68508
Contact: Cleo Horstman (402) 471-2306

Eastern Nebraska Office on Aging, Project
   POWER
885 S. 72nd Street, Omaha, NE 68114
   Contact: Ron Hardiman (402) 444-6647 (50+)

NEW JERSEY
Jewish Vocational Service, Work Center on Aging
111 Prospect Street, E. Orange, NJ 07017
Contact: Claudia Fogel (201) 674-2415 (60+,
   Essex County)

Worne and Associates, Inc.
118 Taunton Blvd., Medford, NJ 08055
Contact: Phyllis Worne (609) 654-0077 (55+,
   for profit)

NEW YORK
Gaining Resources for Older Workers
40 Main Street, Binghamton, NY 13905
Contact: Grow Desk (607) 772-8770 (55+,
   Broome County)

In-Home Support Services
245 Elmwood Avenue, Buffalo, NY 14222
Contact: Thomas Mulvey (716) 881-6350 (55+,
   Erie County)

St. Lawrence County SCSP
Outer Main Street, Canton, NY 13617
Contact: Jack Wells (315) 638-0097 (55+)

144 • MAKING MORE MONEY

Senior Personnel Employment Council
158 Westchester Avenue, White Plains, NY
   10601
Contact: Jack Blanchfield (617) 761-2150 (55+,
   one of the oldest and most successful senior
   employment centers in the U.S.)

Women's Career Center
121 N. Fitzhugh Street, Rochester NY 14614
Contact: Jeannette Kreiser (716) 325-2274 (career
   counseling for women)

NORTH CAROLINA
Council on the Status of Women
526 N. Wilmington Street, Raleigh, NC 27604
Contact: Nancy Mershon (919) 733-2455
   (displaced homemaker program)

OHIO
Jewish Vocational Service
13828 Cedar Road, University Heights,
   OH 44118
Contact: Daniel Cohen (216) 751-3103 (45+)

Lake County Council on Aging
105 Main Street, Painesville, OH 44077
Contact: Betty Worreiter (216) 428-1194 (40+,
   Lake County)

Mature Worker Specialist Program, Ohio Bureau
   of Employment Services
145 S. Front Street,
Columbus, OH 43215
Contact: Paul B. Miller (614) 466-4636 (45+)

Ohio Commission on Aging
50 W. Broad Street, Columbus, OH 43214
Contact: Lee Matson (614) 466-5500 (55+)

Skills Available
1110 Euclid Avenue, Cleveland, OH 44111
Contact: Marge Butera (216) 579-0116 (40+,
   Cuyahoga County)

OKLAHOMA
The Salvation Army Senior Centers
315 S.W. 5th Street (P.O. Box 25516), Oklahoma
   City, OK 73125
Contact: Linda Soos (405) 236-1943 (55+)

PENNSYLVANIA
Area Agency on Aging
R.D. #3
Box 614
Ebensburg, PA 15931
Contact: (814) 472-5580

Delaware County Services for the Aging
Government Center, Media, PA 19063
Contact: Margaret Gallagher (215) 891-4455

Mayor's Commission on Services to the Aging
1317 Filbert Street, Suite 1003, Philadelphia,
PA 19107
Contact: Vince Marciano (215) 686-8499 (55+)

SOUTH CAROLINA
Council on Aging of the Midlands
1800 Main Street, Suite 3C, Columbia, SC 29201
Contact: Randi Olafson (803) 252-7734 (48+)

TENNESSEE
Community Action Committee Knoxville–Knox County on Aging
2518 Magnolia Avenue, Knoxville, TN 37914
Contact: Betty Joyce Wilcox (615) 637-3070 (55+)

Senior Citizens Services
1750 Madison Avenue, Suite 350, Memphis, TN 38104
Contact: Carolyn L. Webber (901) 726-0211 (55+)

UCDO Area Agency on Aging
1225 Burgess Falls Road, Cookville, TN 38501–4194
Contact: Nancy Peace (615) 432-4111 (55+)

VIRGINIA
Arlington Area Agency on Aging
1800 N. Edison Street, Arlington, VA 22207
Contact: Terry Lynch (703) 558-2341 (55+)

Arlington County Job Development Service
2100 14th Street, North Arlington, VA 22201
Contact: (703) 558-2184

WASHINGTON
City of Port Angeles, Senior Center
215 South Lincoln, Port Angeles, WA 98362
Contact: (206) 457-7004

Senior Services
3402 112th Street S. W.
Everett, WA 98204
Contact: Keith Spelhaug (206) 355-1112 (55+)

Washington State Bureau of Aging
08436 Olympia, WA 98504
Contact: Fritz Talmadge (206) 763-3603 (55+)

WISCONSIN
Over 55 Employment Service
1045 East Dayton, #211, Madison, WI 53703
Contact: Jane Richardson (608) 255-5585

STRATEGY 33

Yellow Pages

For more job possibilities, look in the Yellow Pages of the telephone book in the city where you live or where you want to work. If the city is in another part of the country, you can find the Yellow Pages for major cities in your local library. Read through them and add to your job possibilities. List the businesses or trade unions that sound like good opportunities for you.

In the Yellow Pages, look also for senior employment agencies and for temporary employment services. New York City has more than 300 temporary services listed, and even rural Vermont lists three in Burlington.

STRATEGY 34

Newspaper Want Ads

Newspaper want ads are a good place to look for additions to your job possibilities list. Job Finders, a large California agency that teaches people how to find jobs, says that want ads are considered the best source of information. 60 percent of all job possibilities are found there. Get the want ads from any Sunday paper in a geographical region that interests you. Add jobs to your list that sound as if they are right for you.

STRATEGY 35

Trade and Professional Journal Want Ads

Read the ads in your own trade or professional journal. If you have been reading only one journal, go to the library and read others in your field. Also, check the ads in related journals. For example, if banking is your field, look at the journals for securities and insurance for other job ideas in the financial job market. Ask the reference librarian for trade magazines related to the jobs on your list. Read Strategy 39 for more information about trade journals.

STRATEGY 36

No Agency/No Help Strategy

A few of you may find yourself with neither an employment agency nor a State Office on the Aging with an employment focus or even newspaper with want ads that make sense to you. In that case, read through the jobs again in Strategy 20. These are the current jobs that are listed in senior employment agencies in many parts of the country. Chances are that they are the same jobs you would find in your own area if there were a special agency for you. Look at your job possibilities list (Strategy 19) and your ideal job (Strategy 15) to find a match of what you want with what there is. Next, instead of having an agency give you the name of an employer, write and place your own ad describing the job you want. Be specific. Say exactly what you want.

Write a variation of your ideal job (Strategy 15) for the Jobs Wanted section of the classified ads in your local newspaper. Most classified ads are reasonable in cost, especially if you advertise in your local newspaper or newsletter. If you need public transportation, say that. If you require particular hours, say that. If you want a specific amount of money, again, be specific. Remember, though, that flexibility is the key, and the more open you are, the better your chances will be for that job.

Call your local newspaper for the classified rates, and write your ad. Give it plenty of thought. Learn how well you communicate what you want by the responses that come back to you. If you aren't happy with the results, change the ad in some way and try again. Try three times before you go on to another strategy.

STRATEGY 37

Civic and Government Business Organizations

Call, write, or visit (or do all three) the Better Business Bureau, Junior Chamber of Commerce, Small Business Administration, and Economic Advisory Council. You can get information about local business, new business, old business, minority-, senior-, and women-owned or -managed businesses. Some of you will want to extend your job possibilities list to include small businesses. Maybe you have the skills, interests, and values to start your own business. If so, read Strategy 38.

STRATEGY 38

Start Your Own Business

Have you read the ads that suggest you start your own business? Do you have friends who have started their own successful business? Do you have other friends who urge you to give it a try, that it provides the perfect income for retirement? Here is a list of some businesses that others have started.

    Accounting service
    Aerobic-dance studio
    Antique-photo shop
    Art-show promotion
    Auto-paint shop
    Auto-repair shop
    Bartering club
    Candle manufacturing
    Candy store

Car wash
Carpet cleaning
Chimney sweeps
Companion service
Consulting service
Contest promotion
Copying service
Crafts
Dating service
Day-care service
Driving service
Employment agency for older workers
Firewood dealer
Flower vending
Food- and party-catering service
Furniture stripping and refinishing
Hobby shop
Home bakery
Homemade ice cream shop
House-cleaning service team
Janitorial service
Lawn-care service
Low-calorie bakery
Maid service
Mail order
Muffler-repair shop
Newsletter publishing
No-sun tanning center
Paper recycling

Parking lot
Pet cemetery
Pet hotel and grooming
Physical-fitness center
Popcorn vending
Private mailbox service
Rent-a-plant
Rental-list publisher
Safe-deposit-box rental
Salad bar
Sandwich shop
Security patrol service
60+ roommate-finding service
Snack shop
Soap manufacturing
Soup-kitchen restaurant
Stained glass manufacturing
Tea shop
Telephone-answering service
Thirty-minute tune-up shop
Tool and equipment rental
Toy vending
Travel agency
Typing service
Video-game arcade
Video-taping service
Vinyl-repair shop
Window-washing service
Word-processing service

Worm farming
Yogurt shop

Many of you want to be your own boss and starting your own business is just the way to do that. On second thought, we all know by now that there is no such thing as sure and easy money, right? Some organizations, beginning with the U.S. Government's Small Business Administration, can help you with the common problems of starting your own business. Look them up in your local phone book. You may want to start with some good reading. Here are three excellent books for you:

1. *Real Money from Home: How to Start, Manage, and Profit from a Home-based Service Business,* by Valerie Bohigian, New American Library, 1985. $9.95

2. *168 More Businesses Anyone Can Start & Make a Lot Of Money,* by Chase Revel (founder of the American Entrepreneurs' Association), Bantam, 1984. $8.95

3. *Setting Up Shop: The Do's & Don'ts of Starting a Small Business,* by Randy Baca Smith, Warner Books, 1983. $6.95

You can get any of these books by going into a bookstore with the title, name of the author, and publisher. Ask them to order the book for you; all are paperbacks.

One more source is American Entrepreneurs Association, 2311 Pontius Avenue, Los Angeles, CA 90064. This is a professional organization that sells manuals on how to start your own particular business. They have a toll-free 800 telephone number: (800) 421-2300.

STRATEGY 39

Research Your Job Possibilities List

Let's say you know what you want (what skills you want to use, what experience you want to build on, and how much time you want to work) and you know what jobs are out there. You now have five or six job possibilities on your list. The next step is to research each possibility as thoroughly as you can. You will want to find out all about each particular work place. You will want to know what the present trends and the future outlook are for this job. What is the highest level of entry for which you can apply? Who are the other employers in the field besides the one on your list? How do they compare to the one on your list? What is unique about the employer that you are researching? How large or small is the firm or business? What are they best known for? Do you know anyone else working there?

Researching your list is the nuts and bolts of getting a job. Learning as much as you can about your job possibility empowers you with the kinds of information you need for a successful interview and for liking the job. Strategies 39 through 44 are strategies for researching your job list. You won't need to use all of them, but read through them to find some clues for the best ways to learn more about your job list. If the strategy makes sense to you, take the time to learn more about each job on your list.

STRATEGY 40

Business Research

If you're looking at a big company, the public relations department can furnish you with an organization chart showing all of the departments and how they report and relate to each other. Ask also for a copy of their annual report and the in-house newspaper or newsletter. Many times you can get more information about what it's like to be working for a company through their employees' newsletter than anywhere else. Along the same line, have lunch at the employees' cafeteria for an insider's view of other employees.

STRAGEGY 41

Trade Journals

Most professions have their own trade journal. Reading these journals gives you great preparation for a job interview. If you are applying for a job in book publishing, the interviewer will be impressed if you know what's in *Publishers Weekly;* or if you read *Travel Trade* before interviewing in a travel agency; or if you are familiar with *Nations' Restaurant News* if restaurant work is your new field of interest; or if you read *Interiors* if interior design interests you; or if you know *The Insurance Salesman* before you interview for a salesperson's position. Ask your public librarian for help to find the name of the trade journal you want. Give the name of the job you are going after. You do not have to know the exact name of the magazine or journal; the reference librarian can find it for you.

STRATEGY 42

Professional Associations

Every profession has a national association. They publish brochures, bulletins, and newsletters; hold national and regional meetings; give conferences and seminars; and publish membership and directory lists. If you live in or around Washington, DC, you can visit many of these national associations. Or you can write to them to find the closest regional offices and who is where in the profession. When you write, ask for copies of the two last convention programs in order to get names of the regional leaders. You can see where the leaders come from, who they work for, and in which institutions or agencies or companies they work. Contacting a professional association is an easy way to learn more about what the job will be like. They often have free career information that they will send you.

STRATEGY 43

People Research

While researching written materials for your job possibilities list, you will also want to start talking to people. Decide who it is you want to see and what kinds of information you can get before your interview. If your job possibility is in the field of health—nursing or hospital administration; medical secretary; hospital technician; or receptionist in a home-health agency outside the hospital, you can talk with many health people about their specialty.

If you are looking for a business job, however, you may have to look harder for contacts from your friends, relatives, and neighbors to find the personal contacts you need to learn more about the job. Researching means trying to learn as much as possible about the field to which you will later apply and request an interview. The person you learn from will feel differently if you are asking for a job than if you are asking her or him to tell you more about what that particular job is like. One of the key tasks you have at this point is to figure out at what level you can enter the company and what kind of time commitment you will make for the job.

Regional conventions, sales meetings, and demonstration meetings are a good place to meet people in the field. Listen to how Linda, a retired college admissions counselor, found a job in business. Rather than going through personnel and asking what was available, she carefully researched a computer company and decided that with public-relations skills learned on the job in her college admissions job, she could interview for a public-relations job with Wang, a fast-growing computer company. Studying all she could about the company, Linda learned that the president and founder of Wang was having a sales conference in a Boston hotel. She informally met him at the conference and talked to him about what she had researched about his company. When later she called for an appointment and reminded him of their conversation, Linda was immediately given an interview. She got the job, and when she learned more about the job possibilities within the company, she soon switched from public relations to sales. Linda now has a job she can do on her own terms: part time and seasonal.

If banking, insurance, real estate, or securities are your interest, you can go as a customer to learn more about the company. Notice how you are treated, look at the morale in the place, see how workers treat each other. Oftentimes the lunch room or cafeteria is the best place to measure the morale of a work place. If teachers in a school are talking about the students and learning, you know it's a professional atmosphere; if they are talking about how soon they can leave that day, how many personal days they have left, or counting the days to the next vacation . . . forget it! If the hospital lab people are friendly, treat each other with respect, are proud of the place where they work (a technician at Boston's New England Deaconess once told me that she was very lucky to work there because "everyone wants to work at the Deaconess"), then you know the environment is one that's fun to work in.

Locate the people you want to meet at all the jobs on your possibilities list. Ask them what it's like to work where they are working. Be direct. They will appreciate your interest in them (remember, you aren't trying to get their job). Try to get names of other people you can meet in the same job in another company, family, school, or agency. Be sure you are aware of the different levels of jobs and are talking to workers at the highest level at which you can enter the company.

STRATEGY 44

Work Experience

Your current or past jobs will be the most natural places to research other jobs. If you start getting curious about what everyone else does at your work place, you can learn a lot by watching others at work. If you do not have a job now, think about your last job or some of those before that, or ask friends who work about these questions. When someone gets promoted, notice what kind of job they were in and the type of job they were promoted to. Do most promotions come out of one area in the company? Does management come from production or sales or legal or accounting? Any one more than others? How about sales? Where do they come from? Are women, older workers, and non-white males promoted in your company? If you are in a school, a hospital, or in state government, be aware of the past experience people have when they are hired from outside. Is there a retirement policy at age 65? At 70? Does anyone take early retirement? How much time do the people put in on the jobs that interest you? How many people work part time, share a job, or are temporary or seasonal? If they work weekends and nights, do they get paid extra or do they work overtime because of competition for promotions? Are most of the people you work with high-school graduates, college graduates, do they have some college education, graduate school experience, or are they professionals? Are there any exceptions? Are there ways to get where you want to go without going back to school?

Taking an interest in everybody's job, how one job relates to another, and who reports to whom can make your current work place or your friend's work place a research lab for your job hunt. Be sure you take advantage of knowing what everyone on your floor or in your wing is doing. Talk to others on the elevator, at lunch, and everywhere you go; people like to be asked about what they do. Once you get into the habit of learning about work, you can take full advantage of every working person you meet.

Next, research the jobs of your spouse's and children's work place, or a friend's or neighbor's work place. Read and use all of the contacts you've got to understand people at work.

When you know what you can do and what job possibilities there are for you, your next step is to communicate this information to the person who can hire you. Communication skills are the last special strategies you need to get a job—to make more money. Writing, listening, interviewing, selling yourself for a job are all communicative skills. The last section of the book enables you to answer the question, "How do I get what I want?"

PART III

HOW DO I GET WHAT I WANT?

11 Special Communication Skills for Retirees

STRATEGY 45

TempsAmerica's Communication Tips

TempsAmerica, formerly Mature Temps, one of America's first private employment agencies designed especially for older workers, has enabled thousands of workers to get jobs. Here's what they know about communications to pass on to you:

1. **Don't underestimate your ability.** Almost everyone has some marketable skills. Experience, reliability, and maturity are valued assets.

2. **Evaluate your past accomplishments.** Don't underestimate the importance of any volunteer work, business-related or not.

3. **Brush up your skills.** Take advantage of adult-education courses. Many public

school systems, temporary employment services, and colleges have special programs for persons over age 65.

4. **Go to the job interview prepared.** Have complete names, addresses, and phone numbers of personal references and past employers, plus dates of past employment.

5. **Be confident.** Dress professionally.

6. **Don't be defensive about your age.**

7. **Be flexible.** Work schedules vary from company to company.

8. **Work temporary jobs to get back into the job market.** You'll gain experience and first-hand knowledge about a variety of businesses.

9. **Don't push yourself too hard.** If you haven't been working for several years, go back gradually.

10. **Enjoy yourself!** Approach going back to work as a new experience, a new challenge that will break the day-to-day routine.

STRATEGY 46

New York State Employment Service: Tips for Older Workers

The New York State Employment Service has written some "Do's" and Don'ts" for older workers to consider, especially for those of you who have been away from the business world for some time. Here they are—"Don'ts" first.

1. Don't isolate yourself from people who might help you find a job.
2. Don't feel the world owes you a living.
3. Don't depend upon the telephone to find a job.

4. Don't arrive late and breathless for an interview.
5. Don't apologize for your age.
6. Don't go to an interview without a record of your work experience.
7. Don't be sloppy in appearance.
8. Don't hesitate to fill out an application, give references, or take a physical examination upon request.
9. Don't speak with a soft voice that can't be heard.
10. Don't keep stressing how much you need a job.
11. Don't discuss personal problems or past experiences that are not related to the job situation.
12. Don't claim you can do "anything."
13. Don't be a "know it all."
14. Don't act inferior.
15. Don't overtalk and hang around, prolonging the interview when it's over.

And here are the "Do's."

1. Let as many people as possible know you are job hunting.
2. Recognize your limitations.
3. Hold yourself erect, be aware of your posture.
4. Emphasize your qualifications, not age, for the job.
5. Learn all you can about the company and its products or services.
6. Make applications on a weekly basis.
7. Apply for a specific job.
8. Be optimistic in your attitude.
9. Know the importance of getting along with people.
10. Be well-groomed and appropriately dressed.
11. Apply for the job in person.
12. Take a deep breath to overcome nervousness and shortness of breath.

13. Maintain your pose and self-control.
14. Relax and act confident.
15. Remember that *you* are capable, dependable, trainable, careful, and steady.
16. Stress your qualifications, not your age, for the job.
17. Tell about experiences you have had that would qualify you for the job.
18. Stress the contribution you can bring to the job.
19. Be honest and straightforward when you answer questions.
20. Be sure to communicate your flexibility and readiness to learn.
21. Give examples of your stability, attendance record, and good safety experience.
22. Talk and think about the future rather than the past.

STRATEGY 47

More Communication Tips

Specialists in employment for retirees and older workers were interviewed for tips and advice. From the oldest agency in Westchester County, New York, to the newest agency for older workers in San Francisco came these communication tips especially for *you*.

1. The first and most important: Don't apologize for your age!

2. Ability is ageless—your experience is an asset.

3. Check your own company first; getting a job where you have worked before makes sense for you and the company.

4. Write a functional, not a chronological résumé. Tell what you can do—what your

skills are—not how long you've been working.

5. Be flexible. That means you may have to trade off certain expectations you have in order to get a job. You probably will not start with your ideal or dream job, but it could develop into something very satisfying to you.

6. Don't talk too much at the interview. Many older people feel the interviewer is much better educated, younger, and more knowledgeable about what's going on. This attitude, creating anxiety and combining with their eagerness to get the job, causes older people to talk on and on and on. Try to realize and remember that your ability is *valuable* to the company hiring you.

7. Be realistic. The job you get may not be the greatest—not like you had before—but it's a good place to start.

8. Always follow each interview with a thank-you note.

9. Stay away from employment agencies unless they are especially for older or part-time or temporary workers. Spread the word to your neighbors and children to tell

their friends that you've gone hunting . . . job hunting!

10. You *are* going to get a job. Be assured. If you are willing to take the next best thing, you will find that there are jobs available everywhere.

STRATEGY 48

Telephone Calls

Answering ads, following a lead for a job, and getting more information often requires a telephone call. We usually know when our voice is a dead giveaway of the fright we feel. All of us are sometimes betrayed by our voice, even brave and courageous people. It's important to try to speak with a low, steady voice that sounds as if you *expect* the person is interested in your call.

Think of how you sound on the phone. Are you firm? Does your voice sound like a question? Do you sound apologetic for "bothering" the person who needs to hire someone for a job? Think about the times when you know your voice sounds confident: with your children, your friends, some of your relatives. Think how comfortable you are with them, and how you *can* and *do* control your voice.

Start now to practice your telephone voice. Write a note of the questions you want to ask and information you want to know. Be sure to ask for the address of the interview, the floor number, the room number and the time. If you didn't catch it—ask again. Take your time. Lower your voice and *expect* cooperation with each phone call.

STRATEGY 49

Filling Out the Job Application Form

No one likes to fill out forms. And job applications are even worse, especially when you've filled them out over and over and over and over again. Don't be tempted (as some older workers are) to ask the agency counselor or personnel person to do it for you.

Interest and care in the application demonstrate your initiative and interest in the job. If you keep in mind that job hunting is a full-time job, *your* full-time job; then it may be easier to think of applications as a task that has to be well done as part of your job.

Besides all those formal questions that you have to have "right," the problem with job applications is that they are so impersonal. And they're usually for much younger people. And for full-time workers. Who wants to write 50-plus years of work experience on an impersonal job application designed for someone with two or three years of work experience? No one!

One way to make filling out applications more interesting for you, and more relevant, is to personalize them. After all, communications means one human being getting in touch with another. And, remember, a particular person *is* going to read it. Think of the application form as a guideline rather than a set of formal questions that you *must* answer exactly as asked. Think about ways to communicate the kinds of things about you that you want the employer to know about you. Using the form as a guideline, you can scratch out questions, write "N.A." (not applicable), write in five years of relevant experience for this particular job, rather than your 30 years of work (which probably won't fit on the paper anyway). You can turn the application over and write a letter in place of the form, giving the information you know they will need, but adding a personal evaluation of yourself and the job. Or you can take it home and send it back with a letter in place of the application. You *can* be creative with forms. It will usually be a relief to the person reading it. Don't be afraid of changing around questions and forms to give yourself the best advantage—to let the employer know more about what you are like. Knowing more about you and your personal style will be an advantage to the employer also.

Think of filling out application forms as a challenge that you want to accept, an opportunity to sell yourself. Figure out how they can work for you. Go ahead—adapt that impersonal form so that you come out interestingly personal.

STRATEGY 50

Writing the Résumé: Selling You!

Every job-hunting task has a clear goal. The one and only goal for writing a résumé is to get an interview. Period. That's all. It is not a place for mixed messages; it is not an autobiography; it is not an academic essay; it is not a slick hired-out-to-professional-résumé-writers item; it is not a statement of personal and career purposes. A résumé is clear, well-written, precise copy. And that copy is selling unique you to a potential employer for a specific job. A résumé is selling. And the product is *you*.

There are only three things to say in a résumé:

1. You have the skills the employer needs.
2. You have a positive working attitude.
3. You can work with others.

Sounds easy? There's a catch. You have to back up what you say. How you document these three points is the difference between a résumé that's successful and one that isn't.

But let's start from the beginning. Start your résumé with your name and address and phone numbers where you can be reached. Be clear about what hours are best to reach you. Give more than one number if necessary. Make it *easy* for the prospective employer to reach you. Next, write a brief statement about what you can do and what specific job you want to do. Review Strategy 15 (Ideal Job) that you've already worked out. Use all three points to be made, for example, "I have good drafting skills, a willingness to work hard and take initiative, an excellent attendance record, and the ability to get along with others. I'm looking for a drafting job."

Now the real work begins. And the differences between résumés begin to show. Here is where you prove what you say you can do. This is where you describe your paid work, unpaid work, related interests, and your education to document your skills. Remember, your résumé goal is not to write the longest work history or to talk about your family. Your single goal is to get an interview. So stick to the point of documenting your skills. Be creative! Don't worry about what others say in their résumé; be concerned only with how your résumé will prove your skills and uniqueness for an interview leading to the specific job you want.

Tell about the skills you have by describing your education and work experience. Let's say you learned to be a drafter at school or on the job or in the military. Or you learned to teach elementary school in college and on your first job. Deciding whether to focus on your education or your work in your résumé depends on your strengths. Always lead from your strength. If you are a college graduate, focus on education. If you didn't finish high school or college, focus on your work experience. Describe, too, your many transferable skills (Strategy 3—skills that you use over and over in a great variety of jobs), such as speaking, writing, selling, motivating, listening, decision making, researching, planning, problem solving, managing, synthesizing, and time management. If you've been at home for the past 20 years with your children, lead with your transferable skills learned while managing a family. Transferable skills can be learned anywhere. Being paid while you learn doesn't count more than not being paid. Your strength is your *skills*, not where you learned them. There it is. You have described through your education and work experience (paid work and unpaid work) what you can do and how well you can do it.

Here is a list that will help you make a final check of your résumé:

- *Overall appearance:* Neat, attractive, looks interesting?
- *Layout:* Does it look businesslike and easy to read? Are your skills standing out?
- *Action oriented:* Is it full of action with a lot of verbal descriptions?
- *Length:* Is it relevant, short, and to the point?
- *Quality:* Does it accomplish your goal? Is it the best you can do to get an interview?

Good. When you are the product, your résumé is worth a lot of thought and planning. After all, remember, *you* are your own best resource.

STRATEGY 51

Résumé Cover Letter

Whenever you send a résumé, send a clear, short cover letter with it. This cover letter should show your enthusiastic interest in the job and include a request for an interview.

Start the letter with the person's name (or the ad you read, or employment agency) who suggested you contact the employer. Tell how you think you will fit right in with this company or family (in one or two sentences). Say that you have enclosed a résumé, and be sure you include it. Include your name, address, and telephone numbers where and when you can be reached.

Check your spelling and either type the letter or have someone type it for you. Remember that the letter will be kept in your folder providing a written impression of you.

Close with a request for an appointment, stating when you will call to arrange one. And, of course, you will use your own words and language, not some formal business letter you've read about. The best impression you can make is always to be *you*.

STRATEGY 52

Watch Your Body Language!

A prospective employer will not have to hear you speak before knowing if you feel good about yourself or not.

Whether you are aware of it or not, your body is saying things about how you feel before you even open your mouth. For that reason, it's important for you to know how to get your message across with nonverbal or body language as well as with words. One of the first exchanges of communication between you and the interviewer is the handshake. Be sure it's firm and that you act as if you belong there—applying for that job.

When answering questions, the manner in which you speak, as well as your words, gives a message. Pauses, silences, gestures, facial expressions, and stance may all indicate what you mean, understand, or would like to emphasize. Your face may show a question or show confusion or show understanding.

STRATEGY 53

Typical Interview Questions

There are two sets of typical interview questions for you to think about:

A. What the interviewer wants to know about you.

B. What you want to know about the job.

Use your job-hunting notebook to write the answers to these typical interview questions. You can take them to the interview with you, and when the time comes for your questions, you will have them right in front of you, thought out ahead of time. Also, you can check to make sure the employer has learned everything about you that you want known.

  A. What the interviewer wants to know about you
    1. What interests you about this job?

2. What is your previous work experience?
3. What are your weaknesses and strengths?
4. What kind of salary do you expect?
5. What are your qualifications for this job?
6. What kind of a worker are you?
7. How do you get along with others?
8. Who are your references?
9. When did you last work?
10. Can you be flexible in your work schedule?

B. What you want to know about the job
1. What are the major tasks of the job?
2. To whom will I be responsible?
3. What will be my hours; will they change?
4. With whom will I be working?
5. Are there other part-time workers here?
6. Are there other retired persons here?
7. What is the salary range for this job?
8. What would I get for this job?
9. Do part-time workers get paid vacations?
10. Are there other benefits for part-time, seasonal, job-sharing, or temporary workers?

STRATEGY 54

Managing the Interview

Did you know that almost *everybody*, of all ages, *dreads* the idea of facing a job interview? It makes breath short, the heart pound, and hands sweat. The best help is to remember that the interviewer had to go through the same thing, and most people will sympathize with you. The next best help is to be prepared. Get so busy *thinking* that breath, heart, and hands will all have to take second place.

The interview has three separate parts requiring different communication tasks in each of them. It's not all new for you, though. You have already done lots of the interview work in earlier strategies.

BEFORE THE INTERVIEW—PART I

Use your job-hunting notebook. Start a fact sheet for each job on your job possibilities list that you plan to interview. On this fact sheet, write the date, where you learned about the job, and the date and place of the interview. Next, write what you learned about the company or family when you researched the job (Strategies 39 through 44). Also, write the questions you want to ask about your responsibilities on the job, what is expected of you, what a typical day is like on the job, who and how many people you will work with, your hours, part-time schedules, and how many other people are working part time or on a flexible schedule. Ask any other questions that concern you and that you wonder about.

Before the interview, you will want to review your ideal job (Strategy 15) and your list of strongest transferable skills (Strategy 3). You can take these strategies with you. Take any written materials that will make you feel more sure of yourself.

Think ahead about which materials you are going to take to the interview, what you are going to look like (the clothes you are going to wear), and how you are going to get there. Allow plenty of time. Plan to be early so that you have time to find the right floor and room, in case it isn't as easy as it sounded when you got the directions. Be there early enough to get yourself together—to review your basic beliefs (*You* are your own best resource, experience is a valuable asset, ability is ageless . . . and the others in the front of the book). In other words, plan to be at the interview in time enough to gather all the strength you will need to sell yourself.

AT THE INTERVIEW—PART II

Nowhere are communication skills more crucial for job hunting than right now—at the interview. How you come off in terms of voice, listening ability, speaking ability, body language, eye contact, posture, appearance are all the ways that will make an impression. The person interviewing you will know you from meeting you and the impression you make through these communication skills.

To assure good rapport and a relaxed atmosphere you must speak clearly, listen closely, and show by gestures and facial expressions that you understand and are open to the interviewer's thoughts and questions.

In answering questions, pause to give yourself time to think through an answer. This requires careful listening to understand the questions. Tell about how your skills and experience relate to the question. Feel free to look at your notes. Be direct, but don't give a one-word answer. If you think the interviewer didn't get your point, make it again, in another way.

Wait until the question is asked; don't interrupt. If it feels right to do so, make a note or two to remind yourself of a point you want to make. Some interviewers go on and on.

Listening to your interviewer is as essential as speaking about your abilities. Your ability to listen demonstrates your attentiveness and reflects on your interest in the job. Don't be afraid to ask the interviewer the meaning of a particular word or phrase. You must understand a question before you can answer it. Many jobs have a vocabulary all their own, and it's not unusual for the rest of us not to know what some business talk or company talk is all about.

Another essential principle of good listening is being fully prepared with as much information as you can about the company or family or agency. The more you know about the job and where you will work, the more you can concentrate on the interview rather than trying to figure out what the job is about. Good research about the job brings confidence to the interview.

Listen in a way that gives you an idea of what the interviewer is getting at. The type of questions he or she asks are the kinds of information necessary for the job. Does the job require leadership? Team work? Promptness? Training? You can figure out some of these requirements by good listening.

Besides expecting good listening skills and being able to answer questions from you, the interviewer will expect you to ask questions. The quality of the questions tells a lot about what you have learned about the company and job. Your questions should show a sincere interest in the organization or family and the job. You can show your awareness of the employer's needs and how you can fill them. *Do* ask about time and responsibilities you will have on the job; hold off the salary question until you understand exactly what it is you will be doing.

Your questions will give the interviewer an idea of the kind of person you are and the worker you plan to be. Even if you say some of the things that have already been said on your résumé, that's okay. It reinforces your strengths and abilities.

Before you leave the interview, get an idea of when the interviewer is going to make a decision about the job. Find out if you can expect to hear from the interviewer this week, or next. If you want to ask if you are in the running for the job, go ahead and ask. But don't force the issue if it doesn't feel right. Trust your intuition in the interview. Go with your feelings about how you are communicating, and ask any questions relevant to the job and your understanding of what it would be like for *you* in that job.

AFTER THE INTERVIEW—PART III

As soon as you get home, evaluate your interview. You can learn from it, no matter what the outcome. Ask yourself if you needed to know more about the job ahead of time, if your research was adequate, if you were on time. Did you come off like you wanted to, did your skills and experience show through, did you feel confident and relaxed, as you know you can? How would you change this interview next time? What would you repeat? Write down any job leads or other information that you learned during this interview to use in the next one.

Write a thank-you note to the interviewer within the next two days. Here is a chance to emphasize what went well or to remind the interviewer of any idea that came up that makes you unique for the job, or any point that you thought of later but didn't mention at the time. For example, "A part-time employee seems to be just what you need, Mr. Hones, as your busiest time in the office is from 10 A.M. until noon." Or, "An experienced teacher sounds just right for this tutoring job, and my experience with all levels of math ability would be an asset on this job." Or, "After leaving your office, Ms. Hire, I realized that you need someone who can get along well with others in the office; I felt very comfortable with the workers I met."

Now all you have to do is wait. Right? Wrong! If you don't hear in two weeks (and it happens to all job hunters), do get in touch with the interviewer and ask if a decision has been made. After that, get in touch once every week. In the meantime, don't sit and worry. Remember that job hunting is a full-time job, and you can be exploring *other* jobs on your possibilities list, extending your possibilities list, and researching more companies, jobs, and people. So take another step. Expand your list, research, telephone, talk to neighbors and friends, read the want ads, send more résumés, and keep active after each interview. After all, it's just a matter of time before all of your effective communications pay off. Once you find the right employer who will recognize your talents and skills and for whom *you* want to work, all the special job-hunting steps will be worthwhile. Think positive. Think, "It's just a matter of time..."

STRATEGY 55

You've Got It All Together!

You know what you can do, you know where the jobs are, you have researched your job possibilities, and you know how to communicate what you want. In other words, you've got it all together!

As you go through each job-hunting step, keep in mind the advice and tips from the professionals who work with retirees and other older workers. Add to that advice the basic beliefs that you read when you started this book.

The basic beliefs will enable you to dial that phone and wait for someone to answer; mail that résumé and wait for a response; knock on that door and wait for it to open—with control and confidence. You've got what it takes to be successful because you know *how* to job hunt; you know it will be hard (because it is for everybody); you know the jobs are there; and you know persistance and flexibility are the keys to getting a job.

Besides control and "know-how," you've got something more. You've got new confidence in your ability to get a job. You can gather your strength and courage by whispering (and sometimes shouting!) to yourself; ability is ageless, experience is valuable, there *is* a job . . .

You'll see—it *works* because you've got it all together!

About the Author

JOYCE SLAYTON MITCHELL, noted career development specialist and prolific writer of more than 20 career-related books, has always been interested in *Making More Money*. The author of *I Can Be Anything, Computer-age Jobs,* and *Taking on the World*, Ms. Mitchell has focused her career on advocating for special groups to think outside their stereotypes, whatever those stereotypes may be. A Vermonter, Joyce Slayton Mitchell is now based in New York City, from where she now travels all over the country giving workshops, lectures, seminars, and keynote addresses to her new advocacy group—older workers and retirees—and the professionals and associations working with them. Ms. Mitchell's simple message to retirees is that "making money feels good . . . at any age."